MW00649568

# TRANSFORMATIONAL
## STORIES OF
## NORTHERN MICHIGAN ARTS & CULTURE

*EDITED BY*
Mary Bevans Gillett
Anne-Marie Oomen
Daniel W. Stewart

TRANSFORMATIONAL

*Transformational* anthology copyright © 2024 by Michigan Writers, Inc. All individual rights reserved by the respective authors, who retain copyrights to their own works.

Michigan Writers Cooperative Press
P.O. Box 2355
Traverse City, Michigan 49685
MichWriters.org | fb.com/MichWriters

Book design by Daniel Stewart (daniel@historybydesign.net)
Cover design by Stefan Prodanovic

Ellen Welcker's "Nest Pas" was originally published in *The DIAGRAM* online journal.

ISBN: 978-1-950744-20-6

Printed and bound in the United States of America.

# Contents

## HERE (PLACE)

## HERE (LIFE)

# Preface

Arts, culture and the creative spirit pulse strongly through Northern Michigan. We feel the beats along the shores, in the trees, from the skies, and in community. From the artist's easel to the writer's pen, the dancer's barre to the actor's stage, the musician's notes to the elder's traditions, from classrooms to concert halls to nature's palette and so much more—art lives here.

It lives in our lives, in our spaces, in our souls, and in each other. It transcends and is transformational.

What is the essence and the energy of our northern arts? Is it the region's natural beauty or the artists that are drawn to it? Has it been nurtured through the generations, growing richer and deeper through the years? Is it place or is it the synergy of many forces—our terroir—rooted on a deeply personal level?

We have all been touched by the transformative power of the arts. Each of us has our own story.

We also create a larger narrative when we share our stories and conversations in community.

One year ago, at the Northwest Michigan Arts & Culture Summit, we asked, *"What do the arts in Northern Michigan mean to me?"*

The responses sparked an array of insights, memories, reflections, and aspirations that ranged from personal to universal. We pondered place and arts-led community building as well as honoring culture and seeding creativity in the young. And we talked about preserving our stories, raising awareness, and welcoming all to further and share the arts.

We were able to start doing so with a Community Partners grant from the Michigan Arts and Culture Council (MACC) and a wonderful partnership with Michigan Writers, Interlochen Public Radio and the Northwest Michigan Arts and Culture Network. This project is using storytelling—in various mediums—to explore the role creativity, arts and culture play in furthering our communities and our lives, and how our unique, scenic corner of Northern Michigan has infused and informed the works—literary, visual, performance, cultural—created here.

*Transformational: Stories of NoMI Arts & Culture* shares the words, work and transformational moments of artists and culture bearers who weave our region's creative tapestry. Their stories are a powerful and personal testament to the power of the arts and place. We are extraordinarily grateful to the writers, the artists, the partners, the funders and the leaders who seeded, supported, grew and championed this project and arts, culture and creativity in Northern Michigan. You gave wings to the words we share with *Transformational.*

**Mary Bevans Gillett**
Executive Director
Northwest Michigan Arts & Culture Network

# Introduction

What's the drive behind this anthology, *Transformational: Stories of NoMI Arts & Culture?* To encourage people to express those moments in their lives where art has offered experiences of transformation and to ask what role this place, our beloved Northern Michigan (or place in general) played in those art/life moments. As part of the MACC grant, the mandate for Michigan Writers was even more explicit: tell your art/place story. Our sincere thanks to Mary Gillett and to MACC for this generous opportunity to pursue the art-story-place connection.

It turns out that this storytelling invigorates people. It brims with turns and intimacies, childhood dreams and adult mishaps, all the more startling because (as we had hoped) for many people here in NoMI, art and place are integrally connected. This place, it's natural beauty, access to water, collaging air, rolling hills, forests and streams, overlooks and orchards, all seem to tie earth beauty to artistic impulse, and to provide the nurturing ground on which artists like to grow. Though our participants in this writing project make up only a slice of the overall population, they do represent a diverse range in age, economic and ethnic background, as well as a variety of arts—from clay to quill, oil to quilt, poetry to photography. Their stories range equally as widely. We are grateful to them all.

For me, this concept held particular poignancy. My interest in art began in parochial school with a lay teacher—Mrs. S. The good sisters gave Mrs. S "permission" to teach art to us farm kids. I adored this woman, and she seemed to understand that though there was no hope I would be a visual artist of any sort, I was worthy to learn to love art. Bless her. As part of her pedagogy, she shared over-sized books that displayed full-color quality museum prints—I remember studying neo-classical battle scenes, renaissance mythical interpretations, and impressionist landscapes. I observed my first "formal" nude reprint in her company. (Lordy, those good sisters can't have known.) There, on glossy paper, an image of the full body, likely a nymph, tasteful but not quite turned away, painted in the midst of an idyllic natural setting—dark forests, lush greenery. (Eyebrows might be raised in today's world, but I assure you, the lesson was innocent of anything untoward.) What it did for me was to forever link the beauty of nature, the body, and the power of art. In that painting and many others, I felt the three impulses—nature, body, art—all ladled into light as a tangible thing.

As an adult writer, I continue to respond to both fine and experimental art in my writing, but the now matured influence of the natural world is, for me, reclaimed in that light, repossessing and transforming that invisible force into language. That sounds esoteric—but for me it has become like breathing. To look up from the page into the moisture laden air outside my window and stare at trees, to see light on the open field, is to anchor in the world, and also to replenish and arouse that way of seeing. I turn to light, to open air as that nymph did in the forest. The Air(e) of Place is a breathing and thinking song, a way to link my intellect to the body where language lives and can be drawn upon and written down. That staring into good light, natural light is essential to my wording, my writing.

I tell that tale to say why this entire project is so important to me. Place is essential to storytelling, to story as essence—not just in the convention of setting, but as the "where" of transformation for artists of all walks. Beautiful places, natural and preserved places (as well as institutions and museums) seem essential to the transformational thinking that happens for creative people as they work. Those were the stories—art, place, and lives—that we wanted to gather in hopes of shining yet more light on the interconnection of art and this beautiful place in Northern Michigan.

So when this partnership evolved, I was all in. We launched in January 2024 with an Arts Network and Michigan Writers partnership workshop on Art and Transformation. We had hoped to garner a couple dozen interested folks. Over 60 registered. From those early prompts, we encouraged folks to submit their finished drafts. The representative sampler we developed for the Arts Summit in May '24 further stimulated submissions and nearly 40 people sent their personal stories by the deadline. We were impressed with the depth and authenticity in these piece—clearly people wanted to tell the stories of how they came to art, how they came here, how they live here. As we reviewed the submissions, they fell easily into those three categories. We saw that some stories were definitely about the way art had influenced their lives. For others, place dominated their response, and for others still, a sense of life lived here rose up as a way of seeing and being in the world. The structure for this anthology evolved from that natural division. Three parts, the first, a riff on one of the Interlochen slogans, Art Lives Here. We offer these variations for the three parts of the anthology.

**Here (Art):** These are pieces specifically about transformative art experiences. Some are tied to place, but the focus is generally a moment of transformation in the presence of art.

**Here (Place):** These pieces explore place as shape-maker for self-expression. In these, a place—sometimes here and sometimes in other places—is either inspiration or shaper of attitudes and culture.

**Here (Life):** These pieces are about people and how their lives have been lived, sometimes in art, sometimes in a place, sometimes simply as a celebration of Being.

Side note: sometimes, a piece of writing falls inside two or even all three categories. So part of our conversations as readers were about that—how all of these reactions are tied together and tie us together, how we are connected and linked by art and place and how our lives have played out here. So these divisions are merely arbitrary. We invite you to continue the conversation.

The result? A confirmation. Art, place, lives—all interlaced and vibrant right here in NoMI. Clearly, this work that we do as artists has enriched our lives, vitalized our spirits, brought joy to our days, helped build community, help solidify collaborations, and enhanced our economy. All that is reflected in these tender and beautiful stories.

We are so grateful to all the participants who shared their stories for this project, to the partnership between the Arts Network and Michigan Writers, to Mary Gillett of the Network, Peter Payette (and staff) at Interlochen Public Radio—watch for Transformational on IPR, and to Dan Stewart at Michigan Writers for designing this book.

Sincerely,
**Anne-Marie Oomen** and the editorial team

# HERE (ART)

# Nicole Bernadette Birkett
## *Sometimes, I Turn My Shoes*

Sometimes, I turn my shoes sideways, opposite each other, never facing the direction of my departure. This way, spirits can't slip into the shells I leave and follow me to where I'm most vulnerable; my home, bedroom—evenings by myself. It's a ritual gifted in the oral tradition by a traveling author who visited my elementary school in the '80s. A simple act of protection wrapped in the art of storytelling, it's something I return to in times of stress, even in adulthood.

I can't be sure who the author was but she was older, and kind, and had a large number of African folktales memorized that she recited to the rural students of New Era Elementary. It was probably Verna Aardema, also from New Era, author of *Bringing the Rain to Kapiti Plain*, and a great aunt to one of my classmates.

Many years later, on a 90 degree day in early June, I slip off my work heels to sit outside and write about the importance of creativity. I'm taking a break from documenting patterns of sexual harassment and bullying in the workplace. It wasn't the details of inappropriate behavior that I needed to step away from, but the victims' statements of impact; instances of passive aggressive shunning and the humiliation that comes from being asked, over and over, in varying ways and contexts, "Why didn't you tell him to stop?" It was too familiar and too much.

I have the immense privilege of working in a wooded neighborhood in West Michigan. A lakeshore community full of retiree artists who might, if they see me outside, stop by and join me on my break. Instead of an artist, a deer joins me on the lawn, three spotted fawns trailing after her. She watches me from over her shoulder as she crosses the parking lot, wary, but not overly concerned. It's too hot for a predator to take up chase, but I imagine she knows that I'm potentially dangerous—maybe just not as dangerous as the heat. Like the drought of 1988, when my cousins and I danced outside, yelling at the sky.

*Reading Rainbow* featured *Bringing the Rain to Kapiti Plain* on June 6, 1983, with James Earl Jones narrating. His rumbling voice reminded me of the thunder promised by the clouds hanging over the herder, Ki-pat, and predators and prey who waited in heat of Kenya, together, for the rain. This was before access to the internet or cable television, but after Return of the Jedi. We knew that voice and watched enraptured until the Big Lake warmed enough to receive our tanned bodies.

For years, I stood on one leg, the other leg balancing against my knee, like the main character from Aardema's book. I did this through pledges of allegiance, Our Fathers, and then in the waves of Lake Michigan, testing my strength against the current. When I wasn't in the water, I was thinking about it and the story of the cowherder, standing on the dry, Kenyan plains under the heat of an African sun, felt immediate and familiar. Like a spell, or poem, it invites the reader to chant the refrain of "the big, black cloud,/all heavy with rain,/that shadowed the ground,/on Kapiti Plain."

I know I wasn't the only child inspired by the Nandi story to shoot arrows at dark clouds, hoping for relief. And I wasn't the only one on the floor of the library who asked an author, then a minor celebratory, for more answers.

What happens if the rain doesn't stop?
*Then, my child, it floods.*
What happens when the crocodiles and lions are no longer thirsty?
*Then they will hunt.*

How do I protect myself from them?

*Turn your shoes away from you and in opposite directions before you sleep. If you don't, the beasts will follow, and they will take you. But, if you turn your shoes, they will get lost, and you will be safe.*

I turned forty-four this month. In my free time, I write poetry and raise goats. I should feel safe. But, when I took my shoes off to write about transformative art, I see they've landed in opposite directions: one toe pointing at the deer, the other at my office. And, as more time goes by with less relief, I needed this reminder that, as tired as I am, so are the beasts. Maybe it's time to shoot the sky.

# Jeanne Blum Lesinski
## *Art Room*

The idea of moving to town before second grade started made my stomach hurt. We lived on our dead great-grandparents' farm. We had no neighbors, so no friends or villains around. Except in summer, Dad drove off to some high school far away to teach whatever social studies were.

We kids played in the playroom or outside in the yard. My big brother and I had adventures in a tree house that Dad built for us. It wasn't really in a tree but under a tree, and it looked more like a little fort on fence posts. We had plenty of imagination to go around. The lilac trees by the fence were Captain Hook's ship, until we broke them from climbing in the rigging.

Mom always said, "Stay out of the barn." We mostly did. We found the dead bats *outside* the barn, but we didn't pick them up after that first time. When I was sure I heard a rattlesnake rattle, Dad said the sound was a raccoon family that had moved into the barn. There they were, little ones following a big one high up by the roof.

Our baby sisters weren't old enough to go to school yet, but my brother and I did. The school was an old brick building somewhere after an hour-long bus ride. He didn't seem as excited as me about it while we waited for the bus at the end of the driveway. It was tough because we were the first ones on the bus in the morning and last ones off after school. Sometimes I fell asleep on the bus, but sometimes I was too scared because when the driver backed up to turn around on that dirt dead-end hill, I was sure we'd crash into the woods. I'd cried on the first day of kindergarten, but I was more grown up now. The school was so crammed full of kids, someone had plunked a trailer on the playground for us first graders to have a classroom.

When Mom said we'd like the new house with neighbors, I tried to believe her. She told us we'd like the new school that had a big library and an art room in the basement. I was a good reader already because we had lots of books at home and Mom read with us until we could read too. I was excited for a library, but a basement art room? Ah, no.

Even if I'd been brave, the basement of our farmhouse was scary territory, and like the barn, off limits. The coal furnace hunkered there and was a mystery. In winter we crouched under blankets on the upstairs floor heat registers to dress in the morning. I was sure that it was rats, not mice, that ruled the basement. One day when we saw Bubbles, our big orange stripey cat, lying down under the china cabinet with a live mouse, we thought she was deaf. Or maybe they had some kind of mouse-rat-cat peace treaty. I wouldn't blame Bubbles for not hearing-we were a noisy bunch-but the mice needed to stay in their own kingdom.

I liked to color with crayons. Mom said I'd pretended to write before I could read, scribbling page after page of stories on the blank backs of extra ditto sheets Dad brought home from school. I was the teacher and taught all I knew to my doll, Princess, and Teddy Bear.

How could art in a moldy, dark basement be allowed, I wondered.

Sometimes Mom spread newspapers over the tablecloth on the big table in the dining room. She poured yellow, blue, red, black, and white paint into empty egg cartons. It smelled a bit like dirt but, I wasn't going to taste it like some kids did with the white paste at school. Yuck! Mom dressed me up in one of Dad's old shirts. It seemed that Mom didn't like it much when Dad's ballpoint pens leaked in his pocket and made blue splotches she couldn't wash out, but the shirt made me feel special. Princess and Teddy Bear weren't allowed in my art class, but what fun for me! I made rivers of paint across brown paper bags from the store or on newspapers, if we ran out of the special, yellowish paper. I liked making new colors and swirls and splashes. Mom said, "Be gentle with the paint brushes. No scrubbing!"

"Right. No scrubbing."

Even if the mice didn't, the basement stayed below, where it belonged.

Mom was right about the new house, and the yard, and even the kids next door wanting to make friends.

The new school had two wings, Mom said. One for the younger kids like me. The other for the older kids. I'd read enough Amelia Bedelia books to know that wings weren't just on birds, so I figured these wings must be places, maybe like the trailer classroom at the old school. Still, did the older kids have to be in the basement, I wondered.

On the first day, after a short bus ride from our neighborhood, we stepped down from the bus at the front of Indian Hills Elementary School. We stayed on the sidewalk because right next to it was a row of bushes with little purply leaves and thorns, like in *Sleeping Beauty*. One boy tried to push another boy into the pickers, but a grown-up grabbed him by the arm and told him to stop.

"Come this way, second graders," someone said, so I went down the little kid hall to Mrs. Peters's classroom. Mrs. Peters seemed like a happy grandma to me, and a desk had my name on it, so I felt at home.

The lunch room was the same room as the gym and had a stage too, which was why it was called the multipurpose room, we learned. The library got to be its own room and was on the other end of the X the halls made. A sign on a gray door at the end of the hall said *Art Room*. One day that first week of school, we lined up behind the line leader kid to go to art class. On the other side of the gray door, metal stairs led down, turn, and down again.

"Hold the rail, children."

I did, and hard.

At the bottom, we followed Mrs. Peters to the left into a big room with counters and sinks on one side and long tables with chairs in the middle. My eyes got big. Paper, paints, rinse water, and paintbrushes were ready for us on the tables.

Through the large windows on the other wall, I saw the swings and monkey bars and tetherball poles from recess. There up the hill was where some girls jumped rope. On the far end of the room was a door with EXIT over it. You could go from the art room to the playground just like that.

I skipped over to a table, sat down, and picked up a paint brush.

# Roberta Brown
## *When I First Realized I Was a Performer*


A Sunday afternoon,
2:00 p.m. in the concert hall.
Muted midafternoon sun
lights the room.

We are introduced.
Eight hands of forty fingers
invited to encounter
four black satin Steinways
in a pinwheel formation.
Four pianists like bucking
broncos ready to unleash
a torrent
of Mozart, Beethoven, Rossini.
Our hands clammy, sweaty.
Sheet music sprawled
across music racks.

I look up and spot my nemesis
seated **directly across from me**.

I rub my hands
on my black pants.
Playing piano eight hands
new to me.

Mary begins first. Mozart sublimely
sings from her fingers as her grandchildren
watch in wonder.
The rest of us sneak in, we smell
fear and feel
our pulse in our ears.

Not a sound
from the audience
who are ring-around-the-rosied
around us, their rapt attention
hanging on every note,
every movement of our bodies.

As the music unfurls, I enter
a flow state.
I watch myself play.

I **am** the music.

I hit every one
of my entrances, make
all the transitions,
key changes,
tempo and dynamic markings.
My fingers glide across the keys
like a planchette on a Ouija board.
I am tuned in
to my fellow pianists.

We play as one.

Then our performance ends.
The audience gives us a standing
ovation.

And my nemesis
is standing
too.

# Diana Burton
## *Up North with a Stranger*

The August sun was bright and reflected golden hues on the grasses lining the country road. I drove slowly, looking for an address, then I turned into the driveway. The Facebook ad for a writing seminar indicated the class would be held in a barn. There it was.

A row of maple trees and a large pine tree on my left hid a brown two-story clapboard farmhouse from an earlier era. A charming large stone front porch had a sill lined with potted plants. It looked cozy with antique furniture and a table.

I wondered if I should park in front of the garage to the right of me. The driveway transitioned from gravel to grass. I didn't want to stop on the yard. This building was surrounded by bushes, conifer trees, and lilacs with their brown spent blossoms and leaves covered in mildew common for late summer.

A man appeared in front of me, almost out of nowhere. He startled me. Tall, with impressive posture and a gentle smile, he gestured for me to park in front of the garage.

I grabbed my bag and from the front seat of my car and walked up to the stranger.

"Hi, I'm Daniel," he said with an outstretched hand.

Shaking his hand, I said, "I am Diana. I hope I'm in the right place for the writing class."

"Yes, you are."

"I'm excited to take this class. It's been years since I have attended anything to refresh my skills."

He seemed shy and then said, "I have to tell you the three other people who signed up for the class backed out. Two of them just emailed me today. I would have contacted you, but

I didn't have time. I'm willing to go ahead and have a class today," he continued. "Would you like to meet alone with me?"

The barn was just ahead of me. I could see an old saw and a pair of boots hanging on the side of the barn. I started to get a creeped-out feeling about this whole affair.

I had a decision to make. Do I go into this old barn with this man I just met, or leave?

The previous years of my life had been rough. All of them flowed through my thoughts...

In 2002, my husband, Paul, woke with a broken neck that led to a diagnosis of multiple myeloma, a kind of blood cancer. The following years were spent having rounds of chemo, a stem-cell transplant, and several clinical trials. These left him permanently disabled.

His sister, Ann, lived in his home town, and a few years after his diagnosis she suddenlly died. This left us with the sole care of his aunt, uncle and mother, all of whom faced health issues and needed to move out of their homes.

We took many trips to Ohio to care for them and move them into new living arrangements. In 2009, Uncle Jack fell and broke his hip, and after a short stay in hospice, he passed away.

The next year, we took in my parents for what was to be a temporary move. Mom needed chemotherapy for a recurrence of non-Hodgkin lymphoma, but died just seven months later. Dad had Alzheimer's disease, and he died thirteen months after placed him in a care facility. Only their ashes made it back to Colorado.

Then Paul's mom, Lillian, and Aunt Rita were failing to thrive in Ohio. Both were showing signs of dementia. We moved them to Michigan and placed them in separate facilities. Aunt Rita died after a year.

Lillian and Paul himself began to decline the following summer, one year after losing Rita. Lillian died just twelve days before Paul. I buried Paul on a Thursday and drove to Ohio on Friday to preach at Lillian's funeral.

I sat with each of these family members in their last moments.

Through all this, I worked as a hospice chaplain visiting three to nine patients daily in a large hospital system. This proved helpful, but I met every ounce of my humanity.

Five months after Paul's death, I'd purchased a charming little cottage at the tip of the Leelanau Peninsula. I found a place to work through my sorrow, and I attempted to write about my experiences, but I needed help.

A new boldness was coming to me this second year without Paul. I had moved from the "I want to die" stage to the "worst has already happened to me, risk-taker" stage of my grief. I was discovering my new self.

Daniel was waiting for a decision. I concluded, if he wants to kill me, I don't have much more to lose, but I hoped he wouldn't because I still wanted to be a mom to my adult son.

I looked into his eyes. I saw a kind soul.

"I'm here," I said. "Let's do it."

I followed Daniel up a slight hill next to the barn. It was obvious recent restoration had taken place as new cedar wood was interspersed with the gray woods.

We entered a vast space. Decayed slatted wood walls allowed light to enter the room; luminescence danced across the floors. A little window was open at the apex of the wall opposite the hayloft. The left side of the barn was filled with old doors and stored wooden pieces. A collection of ornamental cast iron vent plates decorated one wall. Vintage tables and an array of chairs with table lamps filled the room. A royal blue and orange barn swallow flew with hay inside its beak to a nest near the ceiling.

The most impressive feature of the space was a large open door at the far end of the room. This part of the barn was high off the ground with no barrier to protect one from falling out to the ground below. I felt dizzy as I looked out at the view of farmland and orchards. There was a rocking chair and a desk with a little green writer's lamp near the opening. The whole space created a peaceful ambiance that invited creativity.

The first assignment that day was to write a personal essay on the theme of "my most vulnerable moment." I wrote about the open adoption of my son.

After the class, I met my pastor and his wife for dinner. They were stunned that I stayed to take the class with a total stranger.

Over the next seven years, I attended occasional writing retreats in the barn. I met three women who became friends.

It was following a session in the barn, that Daniel set up a writing workshop for the anthology, *AFTER: Stories about Loss and What Comes Next*. My new friends and I worked on our stories while Daniel served as our adviser.

I learned the anthology accepted other writers' additions, and my son, Jacob, submitted a poem he wrote when Paul died. I was proud to read his poem at the book launch at the Traverse City Botanical Gardens. Jake and I were happy to be published in the same book.

I am still writing near the shores of Lake Michigan. And...

It all started with taking a risk to follow that stranger into a big old barn.

# Judy Childs
## *Small Wild Plums*

after William Carlos Williams' "This is Just to Say"

This has all happened before. Learning occurs when we go with the flow, with life's poem.

We were dominated by male, narrowed eyes, clenched jaw, and flushed face. These were the markers that Dad was going to blow. We silently got the hell away from him.

Mom said, "You know how your father gets."

As the youngest of three, I craved attention. I was curious. Unafraid. I acted spontaneously then ran.

> At three, I threw wads of aluminum foil in the toilet.
> At four, I pushed a fork down my brother's throat.
> At seven, I laughed when my father threw a glass of lemonade at my sister's face.

Our house was a big open circle when the half-bathroom doors were open. When I infuriated my parents, they would chase me round and round. Then they got smart and split into both directions. My view would fill with one parent—caught.

This is just to say that my needs weren't met. After the fathers came home from wwii, I think they were just happy to be alive, and not attentive to others' needs. Communication skills didn't exist. Trauma hid.

Like William Carlos Williams, who took the plums in the icebox, they didn't care.

My siblings were no help. My sister was five years older and too busy to spend time with me. My brother was my buddy for a while, then he shut his bedroom and didn't come out. I didn't have the skills to ask him what was wrong.

He didn't have purple bruises, like those plums, but his wounds were deep inside.

I clearly wasn't good enough.

One night, I was sent to bed without dinner. The crime escapes me now, but Dad was mad. I lay in my twin bed with the sun blazing in the sky. I could hear kids playing outside. I waited for the light to fade to escape into sleep. My mom entered with the early shades of dusk. She crept in carrying something covered in cloth in her hands.

> Hi Mom! Whatcha doing?
> Shhhhhh. Be quiet.
> Does dad know you're here?
> No. Shhh. I brought you some plums.
> Mom! does Dad know?
> No.
> Mom!

And she silently crept out.

I smiled.

I was wild. I was hungry. The plums were cold, dark, and sweet. Instead of a fraught dinner with the family, I got some delicious plums and the knowledge that my mom had my back.

Later, I discovered the poem by William Carlos Williams and felt a sense of deep camaraderie. I hadn't stolen the plums. I was liberated by them.

# Carrie Cantalupo Sharp
## *2nd Grade Art with Mr. Di Marzo*

as if we were under water
that rainy day
we made *papier mache* fish
sticky strips of newsprint
pasted on balloons
pipe cleaner antenna
with bulging eyes and
teeth shards

our fish fins were feathers of cobalt blue
lime green and deep purple
smeared slicks of rainbow colors
beautiful monsters

there were fish with tiny claws
bulbous scaly whales and then
mine—eel long
with an underbite
small spit wad teeth snapping the air
around my skinny arms
a cyclops eye with
toothpick lashes, hot pink

aquarium warm
the room swam with color and texture
laughter bubbling as
Mr. Di Marzo hung them from the ceiling
with varying lengths of twine

after we were done
I wanted to lie on the ocean floor
sink in silty sand
watch them spin in schools
never wanted to surface

that day a portal opened
in time—the fish became words
that swam out from
coral reefs and rocks
flowed in streams

my thoughts and feelings
found form
could jump and splash
in poem currents
that are all mine

# Lynn Domina
## *The Frankenstein Ballet*


The man spreads himself across a boulder, his skin gray-blue, his body looking not quite real, as if he actually has been formed of clay. I can see the vein twist across his forehead. He looks both fearsome in his not quite humanness and vulnerable. He's desperate and alone and desperate because he's alone.

I'm alone too. I've come to this performance alone because it seemed too weird to the others I'd invited. It was weird, a film of the Royal Ballet's performance of *Frankenstein*, shown on a Sunday evening in an auditorium at Northern Michigan University. A ballet of *Frankenstein*. When I'd decided to attend, I figured it would be either awful or astonishing. I'm not a particular fan of the novel, though I've found some contemporary responses to it intriguing ("intriguing"—a useful word that doesn't mean I exactly *like* them). I can easily imagine Frankenstein as an opera—everything is always so extreme in an opera. But a ballet? A dance that so emphasizes grace and beauty? Power lies beneath that grace and beauty, though, and this ballet foregrounded it. It was a powerful performance, revealing the power of the human form telling a story about horror.

The monster in *Frankenstein*, sometimes called more in-nocuously the "creature," is so monstrous because he's almost human. If he were radically different from us, we might find him interesting or curious or even fearsome, but we wouldn't find him monstrous. He's frightening because he is so similar to us. And he's frightening because he longs for connection with us. The full plot is much more complicated of course, but that's what I recognized throughout the performance, the monster's desire for connection, companionship, the assurance that he won't live entirely and permanently isolated from other beings.

Afterward, I felt drained and disoriented. I'm pretty sure I walked out of the auditorium like a normal human being, but I felt like I was staggering, barely able to stand upright. How do the dancers do that, I wondered. How do they not collapse from the emotional outlay? I imagined a man, the dancer, leaving the theater, wearing a long gray tweed coat, walking out onto a dark city street, a marquee above him promoting his performance, the man turning left and out of the frame. How could he do that when I could barely walk from my seat to my car now without stumbling?

I wanted to see the ballet again. I wanted to understand how the dancers had affected me so, what they'd done with their bodies, through their gestures and expressions, to persuade me that I was both the monster and his creator and that I was yet still myself. I still want to see it again and again. I once might have thought that if only I could understand the monster's emptiness, I could understand and then fill my own. After experiencing the film, I realized that this story is so honest because it reveals human longing without offering any assurances of eventual fulfillment or happiness or even just contentment. Earlier that afternoon, I'd thought I was simply looking for intellectual stimulation. I'd thought the ballet would merely illustrate the novel. Whether awful or astonishing, I'd thought the performance would satisfy me with a little evening's entertainment. I'd set my sights way too low.

When I left the auditorium, dusk hovered over Marquette, Michigan. The April evening still promised gorgeous warm weather along with an irritatingly late mix of wintry precipitation, just as it had the night before and would the next night, too. Everything was exactly the same as it had been. Except that nothing, for me, would ever be the same again.

# Kris Kunz
## *To Shape a World*

We had our own easel, paint, smock.
We had our own space to stand
and we could paint anything we wanted.

With my dad's shirt like a ballgown
paint brush a scepter
I ruled my kingdom.

Every day I made roads
black, two-inch wide zigzagging stripes
bird's eye view      aerial.

Every day I took my picture home
taped it to the others, stripes connecting
and ran my plastic horses along them

through green puffs of trees
to blue lines of streams and rivers
by the rectangle roofs of houses.

The teacher called my mother
worried about these blobs, shapes, snakes
wondered if something was *going on.*

My mother explained about the horses.

My mother asked me to paint something else
the next day and I did.
A big round blue lake that filled the paper

and her little round head, brown
standing on the shore near the road
where we could wave as I galloped by.

# Alison Lake
## *Listening to Faun after Another Miscarriage*

The heaviness of the empty house
compresses my back. The hollow
of my womb doubles me over
into a C. The layer of dust
on the unforgiving couch
adds even more weight. All light
is outside the windows, grimy
and smeared with last night's rain.

The horn comes first, then
the cry of a raven pierces through
the speakers, the walls,
the floor, my fog. The drums
begin their consistent beating,
speed my pulse as the foreign words lilt
through the dim world and travel
insistently into my hungry ears.

Something wells up inside, pushes
careens through a body that once
held only myself. For an improbable
moment my limbs move and a ragged
smile forms on dry, unaccustomed lips.
And the dust motes dance

with me and the light brightens,
breaks across the glass,
lies across the black back
of my sleeping cat. She minds
not at all as I whirl around the room.

# Alison Lake

## *Not Following Directions at the Kalamazoo Institute of Arts*

The clay was soft and cool
as the night. I could not shape it
into the hard, burning sun.

I spent all week waiting
for Saturday. Dad would clip
us, my sisters and me, into the car
so gently used it still smelled new,
All Things Considered, brought to us
by radio waves, as we headed downtown.

In the basement, the high windows filtered
whatever light came from outside. The clay
absorbed the light, the grit not reflecting.
With my child's fingers I shaped
the moon flat, pressing the ridged edge
of the shell into its sides so they undulated like the sea.

In the room I was the clay, forming myself.
I could forget the lunch table,
empty but for me, the question
about whether my parents should know
how Grandpa touched me sometimes,
how every dinner ended with my tears.

I crumpled the newspaper and placed it
underneath, to give my moon kind cheeks;
a small mouth, three curls of clay; eyes closed,
with lashes resting against the swell; a nose
not too prominent, but enough. Begrudgingly,
I cut out shapes, punched holes in the moon's aura.

The next week it had been fired, malleable
and easily ripped had hardened to stone.
The twine hurt my fingers as I threaded
the pieces through, made it a wind chime.
In her forest garden, my mother hung
it from a tree until the twine rotted.

The moon fell upon the moss and ferns,
breaking, as if enough rain would turn
it back into the earth.

# Candace Lee
## *Foundling Found*

Vivaldi reclaims bodies
even from where we sat
yes, below the pines
baton blocked by coattails

as an audience pursing lips
embouchures caught off guard
tightlacing all vibrato while
puckers to steady holding note.

Our hands stung, clapped out
the applause so deafening
thrums from practice huts to lake
but silence sped us home.

Easier in another life
instruments, our playmates
adrenaline-boost onstage
by repartee, baroque's life blood.

Tonight no legato throb
post our presto jaunt in bed
only as you later snored
did my jaw unclench

sank deeply, rode your rumble
drifting toward Debussy
began to search once again
for oboe reeds, an abandoned horn.

Roamed among plantations
for bamboo culms
in fields in southeast France
ached for reeds with promise

heart enough and backbone
whittled tips responsive
to surf La Mer's steep waves
until tongue trips, bearings lost

sense grenadilla cracking
woodwind full of hissing faults
can scarcely breathe
spittle holing up in keys.

Then hear the lapping lakeside
when you roll aside
I float up toward registers
through vents, whimpers draw me

among the dust, flakes of moth
an ancient trunk gapes deep
braided rug lay there
rid like afterbirth

its matted weave raked off
tapered oboe carmine-streaked
varicosed, metal bridled.

You say my mouth fell open
a gasp as I woke
loose jawed and flushed

puffing out with unbound thrusts
whelps working free
instilled in me
a newborn's shrill retort.

# John Flesher
## *I Have a Voice*

My mouth felt as dry as a dune in the desert; my limbs were weak and sweat oozed from every pore. I was about to stand before the high school humanities class in faded jeans, ragged plaid shirt and straw hat while singing and dancing to a folk ditty from the antebellum South. An excruciating assignment for a shy sixteen-year-old who had never sung alone in public. Compounding the misery, a beautiful girl on whom I had a secret crush would witness this farce, obliterating any possibility of her considering me cool and date-worthy.

Heaven granted a wisp of mercy in the unlikely form of an oscillating fan. Not only did it propel fresh air through an open window on a stifling North Carolina afternoon; it also wafted the aroma of McDonald's fries that a roguish buddy had sneaked off campus to buy, smuggled into the classroom and quickly slipped back into his satchel when the teachers arrived before he could wolf them down. His predicament made me snicker at the moment of truth, slightly easing the tension as I shuffled forward, gripping a curve-handled cane that was my lone prop. Our desk chairs were arranged in a circle against yellowish cinder block walls; expectant faces surrounded me. My mind went blank but I had rehearsed enough to mechanically grin and launch into the song—and having started, I found that something unseen propelled me forward so that with each note and verse and twirl I gained confidence and I wouldn't say I enjoyed it but by the time I belted out the chorus for the last time, tossed the cane and caught it in midair, the audience whooped and applauded and

I made a sweeping bow and caught her eye and she smiled at me, a radiant sunbeam framed by dark, flowing tresses.

"You have a *voice*, John," she said later.

It would have been quite the story had I become a famous singer and married the girl. Neither happened, of course. But a seed had been planted.

I have a voice? Really?

It made no sense.

Why would a journalist who had penned college newspaper editorials on weighty national affairs, covered North Carolina politics for a global wire service, lobbied for a transfer to Washington—and finally gotten it—abandon the nation's capital less than three years later to become a roving correspondent in some Michigan backwater called Traverse City? I must have screwed up and been banished. Rumors swirled among colleagues I'd left behind.

What they could not fathom in that land of marble monuments was the majesty of towering sugar maples and white pines creaking in the breeze on a subzero January afternoon; the sun reflecting almost blindingly off knee-deep snowdrifts; the sublime quietude of the Upper Peninsula forest where I knelt beside a semiconscious moose calf, stroked its bristly, dark brown fur and peered at its uncomprehending eyes, glazed from the tranquilizer dart shot into its rump. Scientists were trying to determine why the region's moose population was stagnating, and now a biologist drew blood with a syringe while others took measurements, counted teeth and fastened a red identification tag to the velvety right ear. The frigid air was almost painful to breathe, my feet were numb and I struggled to jot notes with trembling fingers. The examination completed, the calf staggered to its feet, gave a steamy snort and toddled to its mother hovering restlessly a short distance away. I glimpsed them gliding into the shadows. It was a thing of beauty. It was my story to tell.

I have a voice.

This was why I moved here. It was more than a change of scenery and lifestyle. Something told me that northern Michigan was where my writing might learn to sing. The stories were there. True stories about animals, trees, water and the people living among them, working and playing, building and destroying, reproducing and dying. I had to sharpen my vision and tune out the background noise so I could see and hear them clearly, then craft prose doing them justice.

At times, those with the best stories hesitated to share them. Skeptics feared I was one of those mainstream media types with an agenda, or that I—or my readers—simply wouldn't understand. Yet patience and respect opened doors. I was invited to a sacred Native American sweat lodge ceremony; visited the Edmund Fitzgerald gravesite in Lake Superior's cold darkness aboard a tiny submarine; lodged with two Catholic monks converting a one-room schoolhouse into a monastery; listened as weeping survivors mourned loved ones lost to shootings, fires and crashes; struggled to understand the fears of angry militiamen stockpiling guns and bullets.

The natural world's tales, meanwhile, were by turns playful, exuberant, melancholy and tragic, illustrated most vividly by the Great Lakes, which so enchanted me that I convinced my editors I should cover them regularly as a "beat." I delighted in the northlands' resplendence but found that it masked old wounds and revealed new dangers. Instead of cozy blankets, winter snows increasingly resembled threadbare sheets. Stately ash trees, ravaged by invasive beetles, became skeletons. Plastics and poisons sickened waters and killed fish. Extinction stalked bats, bees, birds, butterflies.

Yet beauty and goodness persisted: in the white trillium carpets heralding spring's arrival; in the piping plover and the Kirtland's warbler, delicate survivors that migrated back each summer to raise their young on beaches and beneath jack pines; in shelters and church kitchens that welcomed the homeless and hungry. And in the arts—the writings, paintings, songs, dances, plays, films, sculptures and photographs that illuminated the blessings this corner of creation has in such abundance but could lose unless vigilantly protected.

"You're an artist, too, you know."

The literature instructor at Interlochen Center for the Arts couldn't have startled me more if she'd said I was an alien from a distant galaxy.

I was there to interview faculty and students for a news story about threats to federal arts funding. A frightening prospect on the woodsy lakeside campus brimming with talent and zest. The teacher had seen a recent piece I'd written and liked it.

"Uh … thanks," I stammered. No one had called me an artist before. My stuff was too ephemeral, I thought, too lacking in creative power and depth for such a label. Maybe she was just being nice. Still, I walked away with a jaunty step. An artist!

Whether the shoe really fit hardly mattered. It was one example among many of northern Michigan's propensity to inspire and nurture artists—whether masters or wannabes—and those who read, watch or listen to their works.

Nearly a half-century after that timorous high school debut, I stood before another audience in The Alluvion, Traverse City's recently opened community theater, to read my first essay published in *Dunes Review*—a simple, deeply personal remembrance of my late mother and her homemade vegetable soup. It stirred emotions that I thought I had gotten past. My throat was tight.

Was it art? Perhaps. All I knew was that the privilege of telling other people's stories for so long had finally given me the confidence to write my own.

I did, indeed, have a voice.

# Michelle Lucchesi
## *The Tree of Art*

I am sitting on the bed in my small room. It is draped in a dark green blanket- the kind with the silky polyester edgy top and bottom. My slouched back is aching from the pressure of the wall. The stale air and light engulf my breath and the drawing pad on my lap. The number two pencil in my hand tries and tries to capture the pounding in my chest. The lines forming the reach and sway of the dancer's toe point and finger tips. They reach for the lock to open the door, to let the one pounding out. One, two , three dancers try in sketchy lines to open the door, but the pounding remains. The harsh voices of my step sisters pierce the closed door of the room. The dancers lay static on the page while the dancer inside weeps, trapped behind the closed door inside my teenage chest.

While dance was the longing of my heart and soul, drawing was the art form I had available to me. I had the paper and pencils. I could use them. But more than that, I was familiar with them. My mother had introduced me to visual arts many years earlier. Dance remained an exotic mystery from some unknown source, that my heart longed for. But drawing and painting was a familiar experience, by way of my mother.

My mother painted with oils. She would take us kids to the art shows. Each summer we would go to East Tawas on the shore of Lake Huron. We would help her set up her booth and then walk among the booths and see the paintings, the woodworks, the pottery, but mostly we would run across the sandy grass to play on the swings and slides, and climb the giant animal structures. These trips to East Tawas were an annual event for a while, where the art show was a lesson on the normality of art within my world. It was one of several art shows we would attend.

My mother's influence on my art experience is undeniable, but I know it goes much deeper. When I was nine years old my great-grandpa Tree passed away at the age of 84. He was a quiet man that carried the aroma of cigars and paint thinner with dignity. When I was very small we would play on the basement steps of my grandparent's home. We would pass the door of Grandpa Tree's room at the foot of the steps. I don't know if I ever entered the room. My memories are only of a vague image of a twin size bed and walls covered with posters and paintings. He was a sign painter, but by the time I knew him he had given up the profession, but still dabbled on canvases. As his illness worsened they moved him upstairs. When I was eight years old he called me into his room and gave me a rabbit skin. He told me to make a pair of mittens with it. I felt the weight of being given a responsibility.

The year before he died he had had a vision that he felt was a premonition of his death which provoked him to come clean about his American Indian heritage. He called his grown grandchildren to the house and made a kind of confession. When they believed and accepted the fact of his heritage, which everyone assumed anyway, he repeatedly questioned whether they were really okay with it. When asked for more details he needed convincing that they really wanted to know more. My mother and some cousins hosted a sort of "coming out" party for Grandpa Tree. We gathered at a second cousin's house with a large outdoor patio with fire pit. All of us little children were given toy Indian headdresses and tomahawks. Looking back, it was all so cliché, but they were doing what they knew to show Grandpa we were glad to know, and glad to know that he was okay with us knowing.

It was this grandfather that called my mother, as a small child, "my little artist." This grandfather, who painted large billboards and signed them with small pine tree as a signature, told my mother that she was a different type of artist than he. He said she made beautiful things, while he painted letters. But he was the example of how to steady your hand to make a straight line, or how to use your wrist to brush wide strokes. He showed her how to mix paints to make the colors you want and showed her the boldness of contrasting primary colors. Grandpa Tree traveled the state to paint billboards when my mom was young and she would watch for his signature pine tree when on family trips. She learned this was an important thing, this thing called art.

It was important because Grandpa did it with dignity. He put himself on those signs with nobility, for everyone to see. It was in the here and now, moving forward. His art was his connection to the present and the future. In a world where the past wasn't always nice, it gave him focus and dignity. Grandpa Tree would tell my mom that looking back was pointless. The future is what is important. He did not talk about the past except to say, "they weren't so nice," when talking about how he had been treated by certain people. We never learned the details of how he was removed from his tribe and placed in a white man's home. We did not learn the details of the two sisters he claimed he once had before they were sent west. But his art was an outlet for pride which contrasted the shame he had learned to have about his heritage.

Living in the moment was how he lived, not looking back. The past was not a place to linger. He claimed insurance was a waste of money and traveled one summer with young children eating only apples from the wild apple trees. Living in the moment allowed him to train dogs so he could join the circus when they came to town. Being in the moment allowed him to value the silliness of the unicycle. His art kept him in the present. And he passed this gift onto his granddaughter, my mother.

The connection I feel to him is a connection through the art passed down, but also a connection to the Potawatomi people I've never met and the land of southwest Michigan where he would escape to see a lady friend years after the death of his wife. It is his connection to that place, that location, that would belie his claim that the past is of no account. The land was his connection to the past. The art was his connection to the future.

While my visual art attempt was of limited success, and my dancing and music have been wonderful blessings, it is in words that I have learned to use my pencil to set my inner artist free. It is in words that I most strongly experience the legacy of dignity and art.

# Sara Maurer
## *Paris*

The fantasy usually goes like this: The air is pleasantly tinged with the smoke of cigarettes. The call of booksellers rises from the Seine. My tongue is dry from an earthy sip of merlot. Suddenly, my phone rings. It's Mrs. Sherman, the principal at Sault Area High School. She asks me to give the commencement address at this year's graduation ceremony.

"You're exactly what we hope every Sault High graduate aspires to become," she says.

"Well," I say, "my book tour just happens to be wrapping up. I'd be happy to give a speech. I'll even reduce my speaking fee."

I challenge any writer to deny they haven't entertained a similar scenario at least once or…daily. That crystallized moment when all the risks and heartaches, hard work and frustration have paid off.

And just when I'm getting to the part where the gym full of high school graduates stands up and applauds me, my laptop dings. It's an email from none other than Sault Area High School, linking to a survey called Portrait of a Graduate. It asks parents and community members to identify the qualities they believe graduates should exemplify in order to be successful adults.

But as I click through the survey, nowhere do I see traits like "jet set" or "famous"; no accomplishments like "book tour" or "commencement speaker." I see only qualities like problem solving, collaboration, social responsibility, and so on. If success isn't a book tour and a Paris café, what does it look like?

I thought of the idea for my book in 2019 but had no idea how to *actually* write it. I enrolled in a two-year novel writing program and learned craft elements, how to workshop (and be workshopped), how to read like a writer. I've read more in the past five years than I have in my entire life. The members of my writing group are from all around the country, one international. Research for my book was more in-depth than for my master's thesis. Did the survey include the continual quest for knowledge as a quality of success? Yes, it did: Lifelong Learner.

Thanks to me there are about fifteen characters who escaped the pink curls of my brain and found their way onto the pages of my manuscript. I've written their backstories. I know their wounds. I know what they want and what they're willing to do to get it. I've built their homes and designed their cars. I've named their pets. There is a world inside my head. Did the survey consider the playful explosions in my mind a quality of success? Yes, it did: Creativity.

Five years ago, I had a hard time calling myself a writer. I hedged around it by saying, "I'm writing a book." Or even better, "I'm *trying* to write a book." Over and over, my instructors told me, "If you pick up a pen, you're a writer." I didn't believe them. The book wasn't published. My writing didn't make money. Eventually, it dawned on me. I was spending most of my time writing, giving feedback on writing, taking writing classes. What else was I if not a writer? Writing was more than a job; it was my vocation. One of my critique partners, alluding to Simone Weil, likened our practice to prayer. Did the survey deem this singular focus a quality of success? It sure did: Self-Direction.

Now I'm the owner of a shiny collection of eleven manuscript rejections. According to literary lore, J.K. Rowling received twelve on Harry Potter. Will I surpass her? My agent told me that most people write three or four books before they are published. One of my former instructors (God bless him) wrote fifteen. I choose to focus on the fact that five years ago, all I had was an idea and no clue what to do with it. I took classes. I surrounded myself with really smart people who also wanted to be better writers. I got feedback and revised. And revised and revised. But most importantly, I wrote, and I finished. Was there a quality of success on the survey for this stick-to-it-iveness? You bet: Perseverance.

I wrote my book with the goal of capturing my family's way of life and where we live: the "rose-colored skies glowing over the St. Marys in the morning," the "June grass poking up bleached and dry through the crusted snow." Somehow along the way, my brain started buying into the idea that unless I could walk into a bookstore and point at my NY Times bestseller, or until the Sault High administration plucked me from the thousands of other Sault High graduates and said, "You're a success," that I couldn't call myself one. After so many manuscript revisions, it's time to revise my idea of success.

Lifelong Learner, Creativity, Self-Direction, and Perseverance. That is my portrait of success. It has nothing to do with agents, editors, sales, or Paris. Those things are out of my hands. I'll stick with the measure of success I've defined for myself.

Mrs. Sherman, if you're reading this, I'm waiting for that phone call.

# Melissa Seitz
## *Before the Fade*

I ran northward across the Mackinac Bridge during a seven-mile road race from Mackinaw City to St. Ignace. I watched the sky edge towards daybreak over Lake Huron on my right. As the sun began to rise, I paused at the midpoint of the bridge and took a deep breath. I pulled my cell phone out of my pocket, stepped closer to the short green railing separating me from the water 199 feet below, snapped a few photos, and quickly secured my phone again. I turned and rejoined the runners. I had been determined to capture the beauty of sunrise before it faded.

Because only one lane had been blocked for runners, cars and trucks continued pulsing next to me in the adjacent lanes. The bridge vibrated with each rumble and *tha-thunk*. The magical spell of that moment was something I never wanted to forget, but I knew all too well the perplexities and contradictions of memory.

My mother was the first person I knew who seemed to understand and teach magic. Turning a simple hen's egg into a work of art, she scratch-carved scenes into some of the eggs after dying the shells in onionskins. She also decorated goose, ostrich, and duck eggs with jewelry she bargained for at antique stores. Artistic and funny within our Dodge City, Kansas, home, she cast many spells on me as she tried to unravel the mystery of what my own creativity could be.

She also painted scenic pictures on paper that she framed, made purses out of cigar boxes, and created posters for my bedroom when I was a surly teenager. In one poster/birthday card she illustrated for my 17<sup>th</sup> birthday, she depicted me as smoking a cigarette or perhaps holding a joint. With smoke clouds billowing into the white space in shades of gray, I was afraid to ask. My mother, the master of all things artistic, could transform a Quaker Oats cardboard container into a decorated package filled with homemade cookies and send it off to some lucky cousin at a moment's notice. She found it hilarious to write the return address as the "Ford County Jail." When she realized that I could not even make a Styrofoam bunny rabbit look realistic with her expert guidance, she handed me paper and pen and said I should practice writing. My love affair with penning poems such as "Why I Got a C in Home Economics" began.

I continued resisting art lessons by playing outside in the fields or sitting down by the dam along the Arkansas River where I pretended that I was invisible. When I turned 13, my parents bought a Kodak Instamatic for me to see if it would snap me out of my melancholy. Shooting photos of nature and my dog Stinker fueled my imagination. A collage of thumbtacked photos on my bulletin board were my Picassos.

I shot my first selfie in 1968. The black-and-white photo depicts me staring at the camera with an "I-dare-you-to-tell-me-no" look. The large yarn ribbon in my hair disrupts the petulant nature of the photo. I think I was trying to look cute. Memories are tricky.

Life happened years after that selfie. I moved away from Kansas, with a brief stint in California, and then to Michigan in 1977, about ten years before my parents followed. At the time, my mother still created her artwork, but her skills were diminishing. She began gluing beads on eggs in strange patterns. She stared at her tools for long periods of time as if wondering what they were for. In journals, she wrote notes she never quite finished. Conversely, I wrote stories and got them published. I went to writers' conferences in Michigan and met authors who became friends. I played guitar in a workplace band, wrote songs about Michigan, and sang them. I became passionate about photography and went on photo shoots with other photographers. Shots of Higgins Lake, the Great Lakes, the Upper Peninsula, and raptors were constantly on my camera roll.

After an adventure, my mother and I would sit on the couch and examine my photos. Occasionally, I gathered old photos for us to discuss the past, a favorite subject of hers, and reminisce. As her memory became more slippery, photographs worked as a visual way for us to connect.

Alzheimer's disease eventually grasped my mother's memories inside of its filthy talons, and she was never the same. We were forced to move her into a small nursing home. By the time Christmas rolled around, I had told everyone about her decorated eggs. The staff insisted that I bring a few of them in. We all agreed that this might trigger some happy memories for her.

My father and I packed up three of the prettiest ones, vivid with bright colors, and we carried them into the nursing home, and then placed the eggs carefully on stands on a dining room table. We walked my mom over to them and waited for her reaction. She smiled slightly as she gazed at each egg before turning towards me. She had no recognition of her own artwork. I was heartbroken.

On another day, I attempted to see if she could draw a picture, something at which she had always excelled. I brought in pads of paper, colored pencils, and some flowers. I placed everything on a dining table, made her comfortable in a chair next to me, and sat down as close to her as I could. "Let's draw," I said. I felt like a young girl again. Only this time, I was trying to teach her and not the other way around. I handed her a pencil. With her wig slightly askew, she gave me a bewildered look. I grabbed my own pad of paper, a pencil, and drew a picture of myself as a stick figure. She laughed, so I joined in.

I drew a house, a tree, and a sun. She smiled at me again as if the patient teacher she had been years ago. But she was no longer that woman. I knew my art lesson was over. She died a few months later.

Even though I resisted the art lessons my mother taught me when I was young, I understand now that I learned quite a bit from her. She taught me the importance of colors and how they blend, how the tiniest details matter in scenes, and to stick with what inspires me. Nature, my love of Michigan lakes, and storytelling drive my passionate heart. I write and shoot photos every single day. Higgins Lake is my primary focus. I have photographed the sunrise every day, no matter where I am, since December 31, 2017.

My mother always believed in me. She would have danced with joy if she had seen me shooting a photo near the midpoint on the Mackinac Bridge. I imagined the two us sitting together somewhere, examining my photo, commenting on the amazing colors of the sky. "You did it," she might have said. We would have built upon our memories, knowing that someday, only the photograph would remain, its colors fading over time.

# Daniel Stewart
## *The Devil on the Desk*

I am sitting at my father's desk, surrounded by what he left behind. The desk blotter with its padded corners has been emptied of its calendar pages for so long I can't recall what year it last displayed. The halogen lamp long ago replaced a buzzing fluorescent lamp. But my mother did add the small shelf to hold my father's battered leather wallet, folded back to show the compact but heavy gold star he began carrying as a deputy sheriff. It leans against the wood case holding the American flag the Army honor guard folded into a tight triangle at his graveside.

But the oldest part of this tableau—older than the desk, older than this house, older even than me—is the mug. That mug has been on all my father's desks, from the first, a chipped-paint, steel behemoth picked up from school surplus, to this modern, L-shaped design that marked his long ascent from those hard years. The mug, like all desktop mugs, has always been filled with a miscellany of pens and pencils: insurance and real estate agents, banks, HVAC repairmen, garages. I sit at this desk now when I return from Michigan to help my mother, and I've gotten used to reaching into the mug without looking at it, but I notice it now. The shape is different than I recall—beer stein, not coffee mug—but I have never forgotten the face my father molded into its side when he made it, back in high school. It's the face of the Devil.

The mug's body is straight and uniformly thick. The glazes—brown and cobalt blue—are mottled, but that face is precise: the skin is tan and tinted for shadows, with features framed by a thick mane of black hair that blends into a full beard around lips turned up slightly at the corners. The figure's eyes crinkle beneath bushy eyebrows. It's a genial, even cheerful face—but from the edges of his hairline protrude two stubby horns.

In this mug are the artistic skills I didn't inherit—and also the legacy of what I did.

As a boy I accepted the mug the way I did all of the world I had entered, as The Way Things Are, but I did eventually come to wonder about why my father, who took us all to church on Sundays, had made a mug with the Devil's face. Finally I asked. "It's not the Devil," he said. "It's Abraham."

It's taken me decades to understand that answer.

We can begin with books: my father always had hundreds. Most of the titles changed with the years, but the themes did not: Bibles, books about the imminent arrival of the Apocalypse and the Second Coming of Jesus Christ, and books about how to make money in real estate until then.

I have hundreds of books, too, but instead of books about the unfolding of the eons-long, hidden battle between God and Satan, I have history, philosophy, science, novels—secular shelves. Even as I read about evolutionary discoveries and the marvels of life that they revealed, my father argued that God had created the universe 10,000 years ago. Fossils, he said, were caused by Noah's Flood. I read from curiosity and wonder, but my father saw those as doubt—and doubt, as the opposite of faith, was the path to eternal damnation.

I can see now that my father had reason to yearn for certainty. By age 25, when I began graduate school, my father already had a wife and two sons. For a few years he had more jobs than pairs of pants, and I grew up with him fixing the engines of expiring cars and sputtering lawn mowers, nailing down asphalt shingles, patching leaky copper pipes, and coaxing decrepit furnaces back to life. His thick, scarred, competent hands fit around the handles of tools or the butt of the .357 Magnum revolver he carried on duty.

Yet those hands also made this mug, which is balanced, proportional, even delicate. My father had few physical remnants of his youth, but I remember once stumbling across a box in our basement that held some yellowed graph papers with pencil sketches he'd made of buildings, like architects' renderings. He'd been a talented and restless young man, a star football and basketball player whose parents never attended his games, a rebel whose teachers regularly tried to beat rebellion out of him. To see the world beyond the farms and auto factories of southern Ohio he'd joined the army, married a Korean woman, had two sons—and then returned to spend the rest of his life just a few miles from where he'd grown up.

This place a few miles north of Cincinnati shaped him, and it shows in this mug. Cincinnati had been shaped by Germans who'd fled the autocrats and oligarchs of their birthplace in the mid-1800s. Beer steins with faces is a German tradition.

But the horns on this mug's face come from the other, stronger strain of his inheritance. My father was born in the Appalachian plateau of eastern Kentucky, in a town renamed Stanton to honor a man arrested for disloyalty during the Civil War and whose postwar political slogan was, "This Is a White Man's Country." When his parents carried him across the Ohio River, they were part of a flood drawn north to work in factories during the Second World War. They brought not only their distinct and denigrated Appalachian accent, but also a lingering, centuries-old antisemitic belief that Jews were born with horns. This fantastical slander is visible even in the work of Michelangelo, who carved for the tomb of Pope Julius II a powerful, lawgiving Moses with two unmistakable horns protruding from his head.

My father was proud to call himself a "hilly billy," and he remained close to the faith of his mother, who helped found a Nazarene congregation that condemned drinking, smoking, and "worldly" makeup and music. His work as a cop—and as a landlord, because he did use those books on real estate, too—didn't soften his view of humanity.

Yet he was not only what he had inherited. Once, after he repeated his fellow deputies' scorn at "Martin Luther Coon Day," he looked at me, his half-Korean younger son—and his face filled with shame. He never repeated a slur like that again.

One afternoon when I was a teenager, riding—trapped—in a car with him, my father was explaining, in too much detail, how the roads around us should have been designed. It was something he thought about on his long drives as a patrolman.

I interrupted him. "You could have been an engineer or something," I said, "but I guess nobody helped you."

He looked surprised. He also stopped talking, and maybe that was my goal. I like to think I said what I did out of kindness, but I was a teenager and our relationship was at its worst. But after that ride, every now and then my father would pause and say, as if in wonder, "Maybe I could've been an engineer if someone had helped me."

I moved away from Ohio as soon as I graduated high school, to New England and the East Coast and, finally, to northern Michigan, 500 miles from the place that had shaped both my father and me. When he knew he was dying, a few miles from his childhood home on the Dixie Highway, my father cried for me. "I want you to be in heaven with us, too," he said.

And now there is just this desk, and this mug he made, and all that his parents left to him, and all that my parents left to me, and an Abraham with the horns of a devil.

# HERE (PLACE)

# Jeanne Blum Lesinski
## *Silent Separator*

The crows congregate
around prey—poke and flutter—
in drought-stunted hay.
No second cutting this year.
Cows will eat imported greens.

In the once milk room,
faded sheets serve as curtains.
Flies trapped between panes
die under the mesh swatter.
The separator watches.

After the crows fly,
a vulture visits the site.
Its bald, pink head dips,
then bobs toward the sugar bush,
through the heat mirage of day.

# Michelle Boyer
## *Cathedral of Trees*

I was just twenty years old when I stepped from a train into the heart of Chartre, challenging the images in books to deliver on the beauty promised in their pages. In the near distance, my eye caught sight of the very top of Chartre cathedral, its spires stretching above the trees. Eager to see more, I followed my map and those spires, drawn as if by a magnet to a town square sitting directly in front of the cathedral. Here, I stopped to settle my eyes. Chartres. The image before me was astounding. My exploration of its construction was narrated by details imprinted like a textbook in my brain, just as I had written them on the pages of my college class examination blue book. I walked the perimeter of the massive edifice, blocked the ever-present scaffolding from my mind, and noted the architectural style variations at each façade and the heavy flying buttresses that miraculously supported the limestone roof.

Through the front door, I approached the interior of the cathedral with reverence, dark shadows interplaying with ribbons of filtered sunbeams stretching in a kaleidoscope of color downward from the upper rose and lancet stain glass windows. Hope mingled with light in the Chartres cobalt glass crafted by artisans hundreds of years ago. My eyes landed on the stone walls, and I envisioned mason's hands cutting and setting each stone with precision. A faint sulfur smell of limestone mingled with lingering ghost candle essence as I walked past dozens of votives burning at the feet of the Virgin. I looked upon the labyrinth embedded in the floor of the nave and imagined the people who for centuries walked and meditated through its turns, finding tranquility and a stronger connection to their faith. I moved through the structure, as Madame's art history class slideshow scrolled through my mind. I marveled at the storied biblical stone sculptures, the massive pillars and vaults, and the magnificent stained glass windows. Too soon, my time in Chartres ended and I raced to catch a departing train.

That day at Chartres marked the beginning of a new path to experiencing the world around me. Through my new lens, I recognized powerful connections between the natural world and human experience, art and beauty made with human hands crafted from materials born in nature, and creative expression making sense of humanity.

Today, Northern Michigan is my Chartres. My cathedral. My living history book and endless slideshow. I slow down to look, to listen, to see with fresh eyes the artistry of nature and the people in this place. I wander into the woods alone and lay on the forest floor to watch the towering trees sway in the wind and hold up the sky. I walk the wooded trails where lady slippers push through fertile soil. I step carefully in the shallows of a great lake where each footfall connects me with ancient rock worn to smooth stone. Wind brushes across my face and turns my gaze to the dunes, and I marvel at the slow-motion action of shifting sand. Sandhill cranes flock in a field. Billowing clouds move across the sky. With each breath of air, I hear the generations of people who came before me. I cry at the injustices and destruction we humans have caused in this place. And I revel at the way we humans hold this place in reverence. I study my Chartres and from it find my words. Stories waiting to be remembered. Stories waiting to be told.

Nestled between these trees and along the streets of small towns, art and place and community become one for many creatives. I volunteer with local arts organizations – Harbor Springs Festival of the Book, Good Hart Artist Residency and Crooked Tree Arts Center – where I see these connections. Where authors meet and bring their books and discussions to panels and visits with school children. Where a visiting artist in residence holds a cyanotype workshop open to the community during an evening of the arts. Where a community art center exhibit connects me to the art and culture and history of the Odawa. Where plein air painters from across the country gather for one week each year to capture on canvas the beauty of Grand Traverse.

Creatives who live here and those who are in this place for just a brief time discover their muse in my Northern Michigan Chartres. They capture what I see and feel in their drawings and sculptures and words and music in a way I cannot. The plein air painter working at the side of a road where sunflowers tip their heads skyward. The writer whose lyrical poetry connects people to the land. The glass blower who captures the wind and water in her works. The mural artist honoring Anishinaabe heritage on the side of a building. The composer in residence for just a few weeks who walks the woods in winter and finds music in its mother trees. Their artistry helps me find my own words.

Creativity begets creativity in this place where we contemplate the natural world that is our cathedral. A teenage girl walks through galleries filled floor to ceiling with art. A particular painting captures her eye. She stops for a closer look, and I pause at her side. On the canvas, an open space of spring green grass is broken by the hint of a seldom driven two-track lane. The grass seems to sway, and flowering trees dance in the wind, their white petals shimmering in the light. "I can picture myself laying there, looking up into those trees," she says. She tells me she is not a painter. She is a writer. I suggest she can use words to paint herself into the canvas. She pauses as if considering the possibility, then smiles and nods, "Yes, I can."

# Barbara Heydenberk Brose
## *Same Life / Michigan Connected*

> Even when all the important incidents of the past, whether in obsolete print, in MS, or in tradition, shall have been gathered up, and fixed on permanent record; each passing year will still doubtless offer something in political and statistical changes, in the development of science or the arts, which will be worthy attention and preservation.
>
> *The Historical Scientific Sketches of Michigan,*
> Stephen Wells and George L. Whitney, 1834

> The wolves surrounded us in large numbers, but the fire was our protector. Sometimes when it became a little dim they would approach nearer. Their howls and growls were terrific…. It was a cold and dreary night.
>
> *Six Months Among Indians…1830 and 1840,*
> Darius B. Cook, 1889

**Michigan Connected**

This is all true; it really happened. I observe and write about it; I experience it and write about that too. But it's not about me at all.

It's about Melville's Steelkit sailing the Great Lakes; Longfellow's Nokomis, daughter of the moon; Hemingway's Nick Adams at Pigeon River; Jim Harrison's poems and stories; Gordon Lightfoot's *The Wreck of the Edmund Fitzgerald.* Through their creative words and eyes we see the past as well as ourselves.

It's about elementary teachers who introduce us to *Si quaeris peninsulam amoenam circumspice: If you seek a pleasant peninsula, look about you.* (In third grade I feel so proud to learn this grownup language and geography.) We look out the window, up at gray or blue sky, and know it's a color of Lake Michigan, found on our conveniently little-finger-side of a mitten.

We are surrounded by lakes, hills, prairies. We learn to read them and connect meaning ("watch out for that drop-off") to the gray or green and blue color of waves; the direction of the North Star; the feel of sand on our toes; how to find a Petoskey stone with your tongue; the color of a marshmallow just before it erupts into flame. We splash in clear water; look for big turtles in dark ponds. We learn when to expect red-breasted grosbeaks, humming birds, Kirtland warblers, the return of loons, and just once sighted a Little Green Heron.

We meet people who surround their vegetable gardens with flowers; who trust us to drop payment for strawberries or corn or apples in a basket; who know neighbors, and welcome us. The old cottages evolve; they provide a TV, then a washer and dryer, and a dishwasher. We ignore the TV but welcome the dishwasher. We remember quaint wood stoves, faded quilts, and the day we discovered Leelanau Books!

And so—I write about a little red boat, a campfire, a dune, Good Harbor Bay. I remember the colors of a thrashing trout in the Jordon River, the swirling ashes of a difficult and dear Jordon fisher. I write a Glen Lake riddle for four year old Anna. I think about a wild turkey's bronze feathers, how he struts through an open gate to snip off our Queen Anne's lace blossoms, then moves on to hellebore seeds; he's a master of precision. Seven months later he flutters—awkwardly—over the fence. He's leading three hens; they lurch behind him determinately: straight to the hellebore seed-leftovers-buffet.

We've much to observe, appreciate, consider—good stories, glorious beauty, kindness, and memories: another recipe for morel mushrooms, deer frolicking in a meadow at dusk, sunset over Big Glen, packing sacks of Thomasville groceries on the kids' laps—so they can run into the lake as soon as we get there, cherry sausage, museums, lots of new restaurants in Traverse City, and Mrs. Johnson (in her nineties) saying "don't tell me I can't do that!" She did it. And I plan write about it.

## Needlepoint

In the beginning
I decided
Each stitch would
Remind me of you—
Green, gray, blues
And the flash of something even brighter,
A simple rendering of trees, lake and
Our little red boat—
Long rows perfectly laid,
Others stitched and reworked:
An ordinary canvas
If not woven with you.

## NYT Call Me ~ Divided

We divide our New York Times on Sunday;
Some sections—*Book Review*—are good for a week.
Sometimes it asks writers: What are the first books
You remember and why?
Who would you invite to a literary dinner party?
What is your ideal reading experience?

NYT ask ME! I know the answers.
*King of the Wind, Treasure Island, Let's Pretend*
And all of the OZ stories.

Dinner with Peter Scott, Patrick O'Brian,
Herman Melville, and Donna Leon.
(All familiar with character and water.)

On the shore of Big Glenn, stretch out in an
Old hammock—hanging between two strong cedars again.
It's OK to drop your book for a snooze
Or look toward Sleeping Bear, waves and the world's best sunsets.
You don't need headphones, a smoke, or
A wine bar patio. Just a few barefoot steps away
You'll find a watermelon, and bottles of "pop"
Chilling in a spring. Bright blue forget-me-nots frame
Its banks and you might see a frog (leave him be).
Go back to your patient hammock, rock slowly for a moment,
And then get back to what you're reading.

## Good Harbor Bay
## (Michi-gami at Dusk)

Now the road is paved and parking spaces defined,
There's even a sign.

But once at Good Harbor Bay at dusk
At the end of a dirt road
On a shore where Nokomis had been Daughter of the Moon
There were only four of us and waves;
Our two boys leaping up and down,
Then trudging along,
Serious—as children can be
Looking for Petoskey stones and sticks or whatever
Before the sun finally set and they were
Called to come for the ride back to the cottage.

Once!
Two guys burst onto this evening scene
At the end of a dirt road
Their pickup's loud rumble, their slamming brakes
And big truck landing closest to the sand as possible.
Two wonderful men
Threw off their shirts
Pushed a stump out of the truck
Rolled it down to the beach
And lit it.

Two were but one smooth motion
Like a wave gathering up and then
Splashing on the sand

Only backwards.
Two guys moving fast, the fire flaring
And they, running into the waves,
Laughing and totally free.

## Climbing the Bear

Once my sister and brother and I
Climbed to the top:
Sleeping Bear dune
Two thousand years old,
Still a steep 33 degree angle
And 450 feet tall!
We were kids
Trudging up the hot sand
Till we could see the Lake's
Cooling shades of green and blue
Years before (mussels devoured the green
And) we were too old to try it again.

We walked, tumbled, slid, and ran
To to the water's edge
And then turned north toward Glen Haven.
It would be a long walk, but seemed better
Than the steeper lakeside climb
That would take us back where we started.

In Glen Haven village
The nice lady in the general store
Let us use her phone to call
The camp where our tent was
—On the shore of Little Glen—
And relay a message to our dad:
Come and get us please. And she
Passed us each a bottle of cold orange pop
While we waited.

# Rosemarie Canfield
## *Footprints*

I was eight years old when Dad announced, "We are moving." I had grown up living across the road from my cousins. I loved my school and this was the only home I had ever known. All the comfort I had living where most of my positive memories were made had come to a halt.

Dad was pursuing a business venture, he said. We were moving from the small town of Elk Rapids, Michigan. He drove us across the state to Oscoda, a booming Air Force town. Dad had assured mom that he found a house to rent on Lake Huron.

Tired from the three-hour journey, we finally pulled into a huge parking lot. A broken-down green tar-papered bar stood in front of where dad had parked. The windows looked like eyes, the door a nose. There was no mouth with a welcoming smile, just a dusty sidewalk along one side of the building. Off set from the bar was a matching green house. Two ugly buildings.

Mom's response was, "Oh my God, Charlie," then she burst into tears. At that moment, I got really homesick. Dad had stretched the truth about the house. Lake Huron was in other people's front yard across the road, not ours.

This house we moved into was cramped, with walls made of dark paneling. We had few windows. Dark rust stains made the toilet and tub look scary; no amount of scrubbing would remove the ugliness. I wondered what was in that water. I was told not to worry. Mom kept the lights off as much as possible in the summer, because it "created too much heat"; in the winter, she said it was "to save electricity." The worry came when I opened the refrigerator: it was bare. There was one lonely container of water. Mom said the water didn't taste bad if it was cold. The light from the tiny lightbulb in the corner just above the top shelf exposed the emptiness.

Mom encouraged us to play outside. She would sit in front of the TV immersed in her favorite soap opera, "Days of Our Lives." My three-year-old brother sat and played with toys beside her. I found him to be very annoying. I was jealous of mom's constant doting over him. I was more than happy to go play.

I went outside often with my sister, who was two years older than me. Playing outside quieted the hunger pangs, and it was fun to explore. Our neighbors had a cedar rail fence that divided the parking lot from their front yard. This fence became my first horse, or at times it was a balance beam for my sister. Behind the house was a swamp. In the summer, I made paths walking on the water-logged moss beds in my bare feet. I soon realized I could press down and make a quick release; it would leave a footprint. I loved the feel of the moss as it tickled the bottom of my feet. Cool water surrounded them and made its way between my toes. Although the swamp was a habitat for massive amounts of mosquitos, it had become a place of discovery for two adventurous girls. We were eventually forced out, and we ventured to the lake.

We crossed the main highway and followed the path between two houses. Staying on the path was a lesson I learned the hard way, as poison ivy lined each of its sides; I was deathly allergic to it. Before even reaching the shore, we could smell the fish. In May and June, the alewives would wash ashore and die. Thousands of them lined the beach. The waves continued to push these little floating fish ashore. These dead stinky fish had made designs and patterns with their little bodies as they lay glistening and dying in the sun.

Too soon, school started. I would ride the bus with a bunch of strange kids for thirty of the longest minutes of my day. The new school was huge compared to the small-town school I was accustomed to. It did not take long for me to realize I did not fit in; I could not wear a different outfit every day, and I did not have more than one pair of shoes. My knee socks fell to my ankles, looking like two wooly caterpillars. They drew attention to my worn-out shoes. I grew tired of constantly pulling them up and decided to carefully fold them down, so they looked like ankle socks. The adventures of the swamp, the cedar rail fence, and the beach on the other side of the poison ivy path were distractions from how different my life had become, and in school I missed them.

Christmas break came. Once again, I could return to my outdoor adventures. The magical transformation of snow made all this new. My sister and I would cross over to the lake, packing a snow path. Our footprints in the snow looked much larger than the boots we wore. A crinkling sound coming from the bags we had over our feet inside our boots and the sound of crunching snow were signs to us that winter was finally here and we were once again free to explore. There was a feeling of magic as we looked at the beach. Waves had washed ashore and frozen a clear sheet of ice on top of the sandy beach. We learned to skate for miles on the frozen beach.

Lake Huron had frozen a few feet offshore, creating large ice mountains. We had been warned of this particular danger, and told not to go on the ice. Mesmerized by the pure wonder of what had transformed, we climbed those mountains without hesitation. At the summit I glanced over the edge into the black rolling water, and for the first time in our adventures, I was afraid. I slid down and ran for the frozen beach. We agreed to tell no one about this adventure

Making friends had been easy for me before Oscoda, but I do remember being invited to a birthday party by a very nice girl that had become a friend. I don't know how I got to my friend's house. However, I do remember vividly having her mom drop me off. I became very anxious on the ride to my house. Rather than tell my friend's mom to drop me off at my house, I pointed to my neighbor's house and told her this is where I lived.

The problem was that I needed to walk down the drive slowly, glancing over my shoulder to ensure she wouldn't see me not enter the door. My footprints were visible in the late spring snow and trailed down the neighbor's driveway and eventually curved towards my home.

Soon the snow melted and my footprints had become a memory. Then Dad announced again, "We're moving," and we moved back across the state to Traverse City. It was new job for dad and a better house for us. The city would become a place of a different kind of adventure. A new kind of magic.

# Rhonda Sider Edgington
## *And then I'll breathe*

Maybe I've planned it all day—working feverishly to finish enough of my list to justify the extravagance. Or maybe I decide on a whim, the weather being perfect, my desire to go outweighing my internal taskmaster. But always, squeezing it in between work and picking up the kids, prepping dinner, helping them: get to bed, to sports, lessons, activities. I must listen to this other call more closely, it is not as loud as the shoulds or the oughts.

So I grab a towel, throw on my suit and something over it, sandals, sunglasses, and drive as fast as I dare. Jump out of the car at a favorite spot. Head across the parking lot, over the dune, and am greeted with the sky, glowing any number of luminous colors, an expanse of white sand and the water – anywhere between calm and still with no sound, to rough and roiling, as much a seascape as any Maine fisherman would see.

I pick a spot, throw down towel and keys, and head towards the water. Maybe today I'll just stand by the edge and feel it on my toes or my ankles, maybe I'll wade in up to my waist, maybe I'll try jumping waves over my head, if the wind is strong. If it's still, I might swim a little, back and forth along the shoreline.

What matters is that, standing there, I can stare out at the horizon, or back at the trees and dunes, the sky all around me, the lake holding me. And then I'll breathe, and see if now I can let go of obligations, regrets, worries, and drop my anchor here—toes burrowed in the sand, water surrounding me, my mind full of blue.

# Rhonda Sider Edgington
## *Winter Walk*

Cloudy sky, cloudy head, I peer through
snow & wind      whirling thoughts & feelings
park in a mostly empty lot      step into
white    pillowy    drifts.

Blowing stops, clouds start to
melt away,    the moon surprises me
peeking out      against a blue sky
the glowing orb of the sun      fighting
to break through the gray.

I try to leave them in the car,
worries      fears      nagging
insecurities.      Why wasn't I
     more understanding?      Why
did I offer      advice      again?
Why was I      sucked into that
     pointless argument?

Cars rush past on the road,      while I try
to feel the ground      under my feet,
hear the stream      trickling through ice,
notice red berries      blood against the dull
browns and whites of winter.

Remembering my 8-year old self,
sledding at the        next door neighbor's hill
outside for hours    I just had to put some
of the fluffy        white        delicious-looking snow
into my mouth (though mom told us
again & again not to        and with each bite
I would feel guilty.)

I pick some off the railing.
Despite all I now know
about pollution      the intervening 40 years
I put it in my mouth      let it melt on my tongue.
It still tastes good.

# Kathleen Dunckel
## *[A] Sailing [a] Memoir*


Childhood
growing up in sight of Puget Sound;
memories of picnics on it's rocky shores;
of riding the big Washington State ferries to
it's islands: Vashon, Bainbridge, Whidbey;
of water never warm enough to swim.

In college
met a guy who made me laugh
and who owned a Vega 27;
signed up for an intro to sailing in Seattle,
on Lakes Washington and Union,
visiting those same Puget Sound islands
once only reachable by ferry.

Young marrieds
back in Michigan,
learning to sail a Sunfish as my husband did,
and his siblings before me:
tacking back and forth in front of their beach,
on the the end of a tether,
anchored by their father.

Family of four
on vacation in the North Channel;
the joy of quartering the waves on a beam reach,
hand on the tiller of the C&C Redwing,
Lake Huron sparkling, blue and white in the sun.

Triumphant whoops from the girls—
the lake freighter changed course!
Power yielding to sail, no matter how small!
(just a coincidence, a new heading
after rounding Presque Isle, upbound for the Straits)

Then a day with air so light
we were passed by a monarch, then another.
What are butterflies doing out here?
in the middle of the Channel?

Morning at the Ducks, dead calm,
the lake like mirrored glass, reflecting a hazy white sky;
Iron Mike takes the helm, the crew settling in for
the all-day passage to Thunder Bay Island,
reading, cleaning the galley…
Wait a minute! Who's keeping watch?
"Both in safety and in doubt,
Always keep a good lookout."

Early retirement
to do it while we're young—traveling, adventuring,
camping, boating—
How about a nice single-engine trawler,
easy to handle–it could go anywhere…
Oops! can't talk about Stinkpots here,
in a poem about sailing—
We'll have to save that story for another day.

# Holly Lang
## *Sleeping Bear Point at Dusk*

Dusk settles in as I make my way down the dune, resentful at the darkness coming too soon. Tyrant thief of time controlling my trajectory and shortening my adventure, forcing my focus on getting off the trail before dark. My eyes are old and I have brought no light. I pause on the final crest and take a breath. Glancing to my left I notice a trail leading out to the bluff where a stand of poplars gleams silvery white in the greying, loamy light. Trees partially buried the sand by the relentless wind. Frozen here yet growing and thriving.

This trail calls me to it. I glance West to the horizon and see the tell-tale pink and orange glow of sunset and calculate the heavy grayish cloud cover and figure I have twenty to thirty minutes of light left.. *tick, tick, tick..* but I want to see, to be there on that edge so, I run! I turn North and run across the sandy hills and plains, feeling strong and secure, legs pumping, lungs filling and emptying, heart pounding, hair flying in the tearing wind and I am transformed, free! For in this moment there is only THIS! Sand, sky, water, wind, alone yet surrounded by life.

Reaching the edge I stand and look North towards the Manitous, bear cubs slumbering in the bay. The lake is calm and reflects the grey blue of the sky. Turning, I walk to the West and stand facing out to the expanse of the Big Blue and there in the gloom shines a small constellation, lights on a northbound freighter, steaming silently, ghostlike in the gloom.

I want to stand here forever! Limbs turning to stone, eventually sand as the wind wears them down to nothing. To always be a part of this, here and now, timeless and perfect, hearing the push pull of the waves, feeling the wind, rain and sunshine. Night is coming though and clouds cancel the starlight, I am limited by my lack of sight. Reluctant, resigned, I return to the main trail.

Back at the trail, about to descend, I am stopped by a bright light shining from far away. Beams shining across the expanse, across the lowlands that embrace the once harbor towns of Glen Haven and Glen Arbor, carved out by mighty glaciers eons ago. This light shining from the top of Miller Hill, miles away, calls to mind simpler times.

I feel them all around me, the ones who came before. Ancient ones, signal fires blazing, standing here. Spirits surround me and I join them, another among many past and still to come. I feel my place in the universe. I belong. To the wind, to the sand, to the trees and the sky. To the stars and the planets, the microbes and the miniscule particles of existence. Part of the magical, mysterious, marvelous world surrounding me and from that moment I realize that this gift is mine to take with me. It is within me, in my DNA. Cellular ancient memory connected to the past and the future, internal eternity. As long as I have this memory, this connection, I will never be alone.

Later, in my sheltering box of a home, I run my fingers through my hair and smile at the discovery of a twig that has tangled there.

# Laura Hunt
## *Create: A One Sport Day*

I need to move and here in Northern Michigan there is no end to the activities needed to feed my restless body. When they were young and admittedly with my prodding, our four daughters and I approached each day in terms how many sports we could fit into those 24 hours. Our daily tally included riding bikes, swimming in the lake, and paddleboarding. So as to avoid defeat on inclement days, we changed the definition of a sport to allow the addition of playing cards, the Farmers' Market, and shopping to the score card. As long as we were expending energy, it counted.

At the end of the day, we'd hang our sneakers and bathing suits up to dry and sum the day's activities by triumphantly declare, "What a great four (or five or six) sport day!" The following morning, we cleared the field and began anew.

As the years passed, our daughters grew from my willing sidekicks to young women with lives and ambitions independent of mine. Their time at the Lake transformed from that of countless adventures to highly anticipated yet subdued escapes from their busy careers. The perfect Michigan day for them began with an unhurried cup of coffee on the porch shifting with little effort to a cool seat under an umbrella staked in the sand, a book in their lap and a water bottle by their side. After a late lunch, a swim might or might not be on their agenda as they segued into a slow countdown to the never disappointing sunset. And when the stars looked more promising than their early bedtimes, a small bonfire sending sparks into the milky way wrapped up their fleeting retreat from urban life.

Between their visits, I longed to have them under our roof again. I hated the void in the vibration of the household when they left. Upon their return, I'd allow them a few days of reentry and do my best to lay low. Inevitably, my energy levels would creep up the scale and I'd begin to buzz incessantly around them looking for any opening to suggest an activity we could do together. Unsurprisingly, I never got the result I hoped for. Rather, I only succeeded in soliciting their annoyance and a sharp rebuke, "Mom, you're stressing me out, can't you just sit still for a minute and chill?"

"No," I thought to myself, "I couldn't do that." I knew exactly what motionlessness looked like and I didn't like what I saw. I likened it to being a second or third string player who suited up and showed up only to be told by the coach to take a seat at the end of the bench. I could easily imagine that forlorn player on the sidelines, unwanted and left behind. When I stared into that nightmare, I saw loneliness staring back at me.

One day, after being told for the umpteenth time to give a daughter some space, the most remarkable thing happened that I can only explain as having a spiritual awakening. It was a quintessential Michigan day. A cool breeze off the lake drifted through the kitchen window carrying with it a hint of spring lilacs. One of our daughters still in her pajamas sat at the island nursing a cup of herbal tea. Trying to be inconspicuous in my need to be near her, I nonchalantly began to tidy up the kitchen, secretly hoping she would notice me and invite me on a power walk to our favorite coffee shop.

Instead, without looking up from her phone, she made her way to the porch with a fresh cup of tea. Feeling defeated, I slumped into a chair exhausted by an overwhelming and to be honest, irrational sense of rejection. I bowed my head in quiet anguish and asked to no one in particular, "What's to become of me?"

At that moment when my loved ones seemed lost to me, I heard a voice. It was as clear as the noon bells on Main Street church. It broke through my despair and said, "Create."

Startled, I looked up fully expecting to see my daughter standing in front of me, but no one was there. I turned my head to search for her but my gaze found the Lake instead.

Its surface was placid and stretched out in all directions spilling over the horizon as well. Its colors fluctuated as it reflected the varying depths of her bottom from greenish blues near the shore to midnight blue in the faraway middle. As these waters heaved in hypnotic soft, rhythmic waves, my own breath slowed until we breathed as one. She reached for me as a mother draws her beloved near and soon l was floating in Her embrace. I sensed a Grace I had never known before.

Then She spoke again, "I am the source of all Creation. Come back to me, create."

I hovered peacefully in that state for what felt like an hour only to awaken and realize that just a few minutes had passed. I looked to my daughter who sat reading, oblivious to my psychic journey and strangely, she appeared further away from me than before. But this time, this awareness brought no fear. Instead, I felt released.

I looked to the Lake again and felt a new kind of urgency, one I recognized as emanating from my soul not my body. As miraculous as it was natural, a pen and notebook materialized on the table beside me. I placed them over my heart to acknowledge these gifts while chuckling to myself, "Today would only be a one sport day," as I began to write.

# Douglas P. Marsh
## *Touring the TART*

The Traverse Area Recreation and Transportation Trails (TART) organization's Leelanau Trail can fly by quickly, but many opportunities to pause present themselves along the way. Trailside attractions range from farm stands to creekside benches alongside these 18 ADA-accessible miles between Traverse City and Suttons Bay, a bike and hike paradise.

TART takes full advantage of this keystone trail when the organization hosts Tour de TART each summer, a Traverse City to Suttons Bay group ride including up to 600 registered riders with dinner, drinks and activities followed by bus rides back to town.

"I've very much enjoyed the Boardman Lake Trail since it was completed but the Leelanau Trail is probably my favorite," said Janna Goethel, TART's special events coordinator. "It's pretty magical."

The annual summer group ride starts in Darrow Park on Traverse City's west side and ends in Suttons Bay at a waterside park with food by VI Grill/Fiddleheads, Milk & Honey (ice cream) and Northwoods Soda in addition to adult beverage services provided by Northpeaks Brewing and Shady Lane Cellars.

The Leelanau Trail (LT) was well trafficked on the Tuesday before the 2023 event, which began cloudy and iffy-looking before becoming a picture-perfect day for a jaunt up the trail. In the early afternoon, a trio of snowbirds were resting at the Shady Lane trailhead with e-bikes rented from Clinch Park. No one was sure how far we'd made it up the trail because it was the first time for all of us. A young person overheard our conversation from a short way off and told us we'd just passed mile marker 11.

"We ride up in the north," said Renee Discher, a resident of Bay Harbor in Petoskey and Dallas, Texas with her husband, Steve. "We ride to Harbor Springs."

Discher said that she was a graduate from Traverse City Central High School.

"I just graduated from there!" said the informative youth mentioned previously.

"Do they still have that writing on the wall banner?" asked Steve as the youths rode away.

"Yup!" she replied over her shoulder.

Farther on up the trail, Traverse City Central High School graduates Betsy Julian and Brendan Kaufman agreed to participate in interviews conducted entirely on moving bicycles. Both plan to pursue studies at the University of Michigan, with Kaufman planning to start at Northwestern Michigan College and subsequently transfer. It was Kaufman's second time on the LT and Julian's first.

"It's really pretty. It's so calm and peaceful," said Julian.

"It goes by fast, too," said Kaufman.

The trip averages around two hours for these 18 miles, according to Tour de TART organizers. Julian and Kaufman made it in less time without motorized assistance. Traverse City visitors Kimberly Ayers and Kristine Graham made their way in the same mode. Ayers said her bed & breakfast host pointed her to a local bicycle rental and the LT for a good time.

"We left our third day open," she said. "She was like, you should ride all the way to Suttons Bay."

Ayers said she and Graham were on a girls' trip via recommendation from a fourth generation TC native whom they met while studying at West Virginia University (go

Mountaineers!). The BATA bus saved those of us unprepared for a 36-mile out-and-back.

"I was gonna die. I was not gonna make it back," said Ayers. "My rental bike seat was not doing it for me."

Tour de TART riders, who disembark any time between 4:30 and 6:30 p.m. on the day of the ride, need not worry about return trips either, said Goethel.

"We actually use TCAPS (Traverse City Area Public Schools) school buses for the event," she said. "Bikes are transported back in box trucks."

Regardless, there's no need to tire oneself on the LT, which is smooth, flat and well apportioned with rest areas and attractions. Some of the foremost causes for pauses are the arresting artwork, which is installed and in progress along the LT and elsewhere in NoMI trail networks.

TART trail art director (among other hats) Caitlin Early said fitness and creative crowds have coalesced around several art initiatives. Poetry on the LT launched this year in collaboration with Anne-Marie Oomen to highlight Michigan writers with chalk art on the trail. Recent rains had washed away the work of five poets but their work was to be reapplied in mid-August and throughout the rest of the season. Response to the project has exceeded expectations and offers a bright future, said Early, who was part of an event earlier in the summer to bring writers, builders, users and organizers together.

"The event was incredible," said Early. Subsequent public response has also been overwhelmingly positive.

"We've had criticism, like, make them bigger," Early mused.

Early said more art is ongoing in the TART network, including more murals on the Boardman Lake Loop and a sculpture on the LT by Bill Allen that was to be installed that fall.

Enthusiastic use and support for expansion of these trails is a good sign for the Grand Traverse region. It suggests a vibrant, active community engaged in the important work of maintaining and improving connections, not to mention facilitating sustainable transportation and recreation.

See you out on the trails.

# Marsha Jane Orr
## *We wept, sown together in our communal experience of the arts*

U sually when we think about the impact of the arts, we ponder artists, performers, exhibits, patrons, members, sponsors—the core beneficiaries & providers of the arts. Rarely do we hear about those of us involved behind the scene in the administration & program delivery aspects of art.

Choosing that work changed my life profoundly.

I essentially left home at age 18, deserted my family and all I loved in some kind of self-righteous complaint against what I knew. It was the late 1960s and I was on the side of change. It left me with 50 cents in the bank and choosing between breakfast and the *New York Times*.

Fast forward 50 years, I was worn out from all the "good" fight, a widow, returning from a near 5-year stint in Australia, a failed consulting start up, and nothing to show for my life. "Failure to thrive" and self-pity well described me. The prodigal daughter returns home.

A childhood friend invited me to apply and I secured the role of Development Director for the Mackinac Arts Council. I was a management consultant run dry, after the 2009 Global Fiscal Crises retrenched firms, and I was happy to accept my grocery store cashier rescue.

I had all the academic credentials: 3 university Master degrees, with one from an Ivy League thrown in for good measure. I had successfully navigated Fortune 500 corporate and university leadership roles: hired, fired, laid off—all in good measure. I had my marching stripes, true and tested.

But when I took that ferry boat back to my childhood homeland, I wept. All the memories of loss and estrangement came rolling back. I knew people from when I was 20, but now I felt like I was still 18 threading my way into uncharted territory. My family had stayed, grown businesses, and made a community impact. I trembled as my sisters met me at the dock with open arms.

Mackinac Island in the Straits of Michigan was voted the #1 Island in the Continental USA in 2022. With its unique blend of history, horse & buggy culture and natural beauty, the Island attracts over 1 million visitors every year, mostly through the summer season when nearly 20,000 a day can visit. The Arts Council mission is to collaborate with arts and other organizations to create, sponsor, and promote Mackinac Island artistic activities, artists, and programs, enriching the lives of all those who experience our offerings.

My new job was new also to the Council, undefined, like me. Not everyone was thrilled with my return. As a teen, I had manufactured my disinheritance. I was like the black sheep in the family. Still, as a wayward child of a long-time island family, people cheered when I was introduced at the first classical performance I attended. They weren't so much clapping for me, but rather for the idea of family reunification, a healing that my presence represented. At the next function, I recall speaking about my fear to a long- term Board member, sharing that I didn't know anyone. He reassured me saying, just smile, they know you. Another patron told me, 'Everyone wants you to succeed!' How amazing is that? The bond of community allowed me to plant feet in the ground and stabilize myself. The work came on briskly and I was barely keeping one step ahead of due deliverables, but I was daily growing into my new role.

Even so, nothing matched the actual "heart into soul" healing I experienced attending live performances: musicians, actors, artists, dancers, all pouring their 'healing balm' over my empty places. When COVID hit in 2020, because one of our most exquisite outside venues is the Mackinac Historic State Parks, Marquette Park, we were able to continue to bring live performances using cone spacing to create safe space among us.

People attending, Island residents, students, employees, workers, and guests, gathered to celebrate the renewal of life through live performances. Few expected the vibrant way live performances touched our hearts, and brought us together with family and friends through arts and culture.

We all wept in those days and the tears were tears of thanksgiving that we could be part of a thriving community that loves history, art and culture. We transformed ourselves with that love.

Through my brief tenure, volunteers, members, donors and sponsors have come together to create a legacy of arts and culture on Mackinac Island, Michigan. None of this is possible without one another.

# Vonni Sage
## *Art in Place*

*Does place matter?*
*Ask salmon*
*Inquire of Monarch butterflies*
*Loons may offer an opinion*
*Sparrows say so*

Northwestern Michigan's raw splendor is art in its most basic form. Nature's creativity. Untouched, nourishing, expectant. Drawing forth life, painting ever-changing landscapes, writing new chapters. This land of dunes and forests awes and hugs. Inspiration wells forth from twinkling lakes, undulating hills, magnificent birches, cocky porcupines, trilling warblers, antiquated pine cones, luscious berries, bustling ants, vexing mosquitoes. This is an artist's wonderland, where we can dream up a dozen exquisite new ideas while in a kayak.

Congruence with nature is central to my various art forms. The trees watch over me as I nestle in their embrace, animals sing ideas to me, and the sky is my blanket, especially at night. Imagine trying to capture nature's essence while *not* in Michigan. It's nearly impossible for me.

Growing up in the hills of West Virginia—"in the sticks" was the local drawl—I spent my summers in the woods or splashing in the "crick." Many nights I lounged under the cherry tree, losing myself in the stars, lulled into dreamland by whip-poor-wills. I told stories, drew pictures, and shared them with my rabbits and horses. For a time, I included Billy, the eccentric goat whose antics landed him in the back of a Suburban, staring at me as he disappeared down the driveway on his way to my cousin's funny farm. I'm pretty sure his tenure at our place ended with his launch into the middle of the table during Mom's potluck. He became fodder for the stories I told the remaining animals. I grew up an artist, but didn't know it.

Yes, place matters. It mattered to me when I was growing, my creative spark bounding alongside me. Place mattered when I left my rural roots for urban and suburban settings where the rat race pulled me under. It mattered when I discovered northern Michigan's purity and rediscovered my inner creator.

In all my travels, summers spent in northern Michigan made me believe I was an artist. Europe and the U.K. had no such effect. No other state I lived in buoyed my spark (most especially, not Ohio :).

At first, I was a seasonal visitor, then a seasonal resident. In northern Michigan, my first novel sprang to life. Wherever I went, drawing pads and journals, graphite and colored pencils were my companions. From Frankfort to Mackinac Island, they captured lake views, dunes, forests, and wineries in stunning hues and lyrical voice. Goofy animals cavorted off the page. My unshelled almond drawing stared back, grinning. Trees sprouted faces. Oddities came to life when one of my kids scribbled on the page and challenged me to make something of it. Dinner plates and utensils were supplanted with palates and crayons.

Only here did I experience that nonstop creative, expressive self, finding fulfillment in an unending flow of drawing, sketching, and writing. Something in the air or the water infiltrated my being. When I returned to wherever my year-round residence was at the time, I left my fanciful verve behind, naught but a memory, a distance flicker to carry me through until I once again sat at the lake shore, relaxed, irrepressible.

Once upon a time, I moved to a land far, far away. My inability to recapture the mountainous highs of my northern Michigan creative peaks defied Los Angeles's reputation.

Even when I ventured into the hills and sat among the trees or wrote stories about the turtles in UCLA's botanical garden, my pores were hardened. Creativity could only seep through cracks and crevices. Though I enjoyed L.A., I longed for space, pines, farms, and an artistic community. Northern California? Colorado? I could go anywhere.

Settling in northwest Michigan is a homecoming. Whippoor-wills welcomed me the first late spring when I opened the farmhouse windows to bask in the cool air. I smile-cried. The last time I heard their song was just before I left my childhood home for good. Finally, I am home again, in this place that calls to my inner child.

Northern Michigan's natural brilliance includes its people. Here, in this place, I quickly discovered state, regional, and local organizations full of artists and culture bearers who embrace collaboration. Michigan Writers provides a support network and learning opportunities for all ages and writing styles. I met local artists through the Arts and Culture Alliance of Manistee County and rural Black artists through the Manistee Area Racial Justice and Diversity Initiative (MARJDI). The Michigan Music Alliance steps out of traditional music industry norms to declare, on its front page, "Celebrating Collaboration Over Competition." What a concept! Where did I learn about this anomaly? At the Northwest Michigan Arts and Culture Network Summit. The unique aspects of this combined natural paradise, agricultural nexus, and tourist hub are embraced by organizations such as Grow Benzie. I've attended many Crosshatch events where arts, artists, and culture bearers were affirmed and celebrated, and I learned from a kaleidoscope of arts residency personnel. During an Agritourism summit, the importance of connecting with local artists was addressed by more than one presenter. Crooked Tree Arts Center hosted "Agricultura" this past spring. These are a mere sampling, a tiny taste, of the abundant connections, people, and organizations where art is honored.

In this place, art is everywhere. People, land, trees, plants, animals... we're all connected, and here that interdependence feels so much more real, more elemental, than other places I've been. In this place, art is not separate from any aspect of living. We breathe it in the clean air, absorb it in the natural beauty, speak and dream of it. Here, in this art, in Northwest Michigan, place matters.

# Shelley Smithson
## *Wind and Waves of Grand Traverse Bay*

I am washed in gratitude as I see and hear
The herd of waves stampeding across the waters
Of Grand Traverse Bay

Five hundred feet from my front porch on River Street
The waves rush to shore with an insistence that demands
That walkers turn their heads into the thunder of sound

A prolonged roar that rides the gusts of air
An onshore wind that anoints the lookers-on
With the clarity that comes from standing in the path of
     such fury

The harsh but friendly winds pound incessantly
Through the streets of Elk Rapids
The frantic flag struggling to stand tall

In this April afternoon that gushes with momentum
I notice the robin's nest mounted near the crest of the
     bare maple
Bobbing in the wind but yet fiercely attached

The former avian home now part of the artwork
Of the tree's sculpted branches brushing against the sky
Like conductor's hands guiding nature's notes

And I know that this strength of force coming in from
    parts unseen
Does not thrash me down or drown me
But emboldens me to search for what I sometimes think
    not possible

# Minnie Wabanimkee
## *Honoring and Sharing Traditions*

My name is Minnie Wabanimkee and I am a full-blood Odawa from northern Michigan. I live on my reservation, belonging to the Grand Traverse Band of Ottawas and Chippewas. I feel blessed to live on the same grounds where my ancestors lived for centuries.

I am a photographer, journalist, and artist. I have spent my lifetime documenting the life of Native people in the Midwest area, starting off as a photographer for the Traverse City Record-Eagle. Many of my photos have been exhibited in state and national museums. I am a recipient of the Robert F. Kennedy Journalism Award for Excellence in Photojournalism. I have several publications, including *Contemporary Great Lakes Powwow Regalia "Nda Maamawigaami (Together We Dance)"* and several smaller publications.

Documenting native people has been my life's work and salvation. My legacy will be in my photographs long after I am gone, and I take comfort in that. Meaningful work has always been my objective, and I am honing my skills in videography, another valuable medium to tell our stories. Currently I am working on a collaborative effort with four museums on Native quillwork artists.

My life as a native Odawa is typical in that I lived with my parents and my extended family until school age when I was sent away with my three brothers to a Catholic boarding school in Harbor Springs. Summers were spent at home, and I have very fond memories of listening to my grandparents' stories of growing up in Peshawbestown and spending summers with my parents on the Manitou islands. But these happy times were always interrupted by my return to boarding school

The horrors inflicted on me and hundreds of innocent Indian children are all true, for I witnessed much abuse myself. The beatings and demeaning were real. My older brother died at a young age from alcoholism, tormented by those memories.

I feel that my images speak to the injustice in Indian Country. But also to the beauty and the reality of Indian life in these times. Many of my photographs tell a story about loss, hardship, abuse in Native communities. Others capture our joy in dance and creating Native art.

I believe my unique creative effort brings awareness to all that is current about life in Indian Country. It is my hope that you see some value in my work.

# Ellen Welcker
## *Nest Pas*

> *One can't depend on people who just let things happen.*
> –Tove Jansson, *The Summer Book*

A parasite attaches itself to its host and is well-adapted to this mode of transport. It's true you prefer to let external forces etch an evolving course over the millennia of your life. You're like a burr, a tumbleweed, a hitchhiker that way. When you roll to a stop, you stand gaping. Two thousand miles. There are unfamiliar birds here, and this morning you'll enter your room to find a frog, covered in lint, vocal sac pulsing. What here is here? Your skin crawls.

Your skin crawls because of the ticks. The thought of them, really—more accurate to say your mind crawls with ticks. On the pie chart it's 25% ticks. On the Venn diagram, it's action / ticks / thought. On a bar graph only eating and sleeping outrank them. To say you haven't seen one yet is to admit how worried you are that they've gone undetected by you. Your newcomer's eyes. Perhaps they are burrowed mouth-deep right now in the peachy flesh of the children.

Your own skin, with its formerly unconcerning constellations of freckles and moles, now seems a sleeper cell for disease-carrying sanguisuges. Your skin: you doubt it. You doubt your own skin. All night, ticks phantom your pits, your scalp, your crotch. The ghost of their latching wakes you, a tingling so close to desire—the way the milk lets down, or used to. It matters not whether the babies are near enough for nursing, or even babies anymore. You can imagine them.

The way you imagine that in this low, flat place, clouds *are* mountains. Such vertical poof and towering. Inside each cumulo a billion possibilities and in each possibility a million more. It's a real pyramid scheme. Near the bottom are the five species of ticks. All newcomers, like you. The climate increasingly perfect for you all.

Every day you read one chapter of *The Summer Book*. You love it unabashedly. You love its dead mother and its grandmother who lies to the child, sometimes kindly. You savor it. Like all books, you are learning how to die by it. This is often how you feel twenty pages into a book. But still true.

All night you lie in the liminal space between sleep and waking, your body attuned to sensation, crawling, recalling. How just breathing in the same darkness as another lit you up from within, how a brush or a shift in the bed did things to you. The hairs rising from their follicles. How even inside those slick pink coils of your brain, you got sent. Bit. Spent. You move through your waking hours a paper doll, blood-sucked, half-wracked, possessed.

The smaller child picks up on your angst. Can you promise him endless safety and security, as he demands? Promise and you can't. Promise and you can't. You check your bodies and check your bodies and check your bodies and are dismayed upon waking to find the dog, that vector, has slunk up onto the child's bed in the night.

Here it is impossible to get up high, to gain a view, to see beyond one's narrow path through the canopy, and this is why people love the great lake: because at its shore, finally, they can see all the way to the horizon. They can feel both tiny and infinite again, like a tick.

Every time you look at the map, the map is mostly water. It is a lake or the map is the sea. The water is water or is it the land. The land blinks like an eye in the sun; the water is water, you float like a mote. The land is a wad of used up plastic, a continent, a shelf adrift. Every time. You look. At the map, the map, the map.

Despite yourself you grow fond of this water. You imagine it frozen in wicked waves of deep January glacial blue. All the ticks suspended in ice like fossils.

Try not to dwell on the image forming in your mind: you and the tick locked in a DNA-shaped twist of anthropocentric parasitic relation. Risk and desire tangled up like legs.

You sit down at the computer and realize you have forgotten what you'd thought to sit down and write. Fruit flies swarm your head like a rotting peach. Moths flutter helplessly at the screen. Outside are the ticks, like secrets on their bent stems, reaching for you as you think and think. It's called "questing."

You ask your child to run down and pull up the sign by the mailbox: No Trespassing. The sign, when he returns with it, is metal and labeled as cancer-causing. You aren't sure what to do with this information. Is it off-gassing now? Cancerous how? You cut and re-organize its letters to read: n'est-ce pas? Though you will have to locate -ce. Nest pas, then. Nest in the negative. You hammer the sign into the ecotone: the three-foot-or-so transitional zone between the open space of the meadow and the chestnut orchard. Ecotones are the preferred habitat of many ticks. The sign is for them, maybe. No nest for you.

"Is it an exhibit?" asks the grandmother. The little piles of rocks. Shells. Treasures from ventures into the forest. Beach sculptures of found materials. Fairy homes. There's a knap-weed exhibit in the field. A dry gulch exhibit in the driveway. Whatever you are looking for is what you see, she says, and it's true, mostly.

Ticks are like raisins. They dry out and fall to the bottom of your bag. They are covered in sand. They climb tall grasses and wave their arms like concertgoers. They wear sunglasses, even inside. Their dance moves are synchronized as a boy band. Together, they can weaken a moose—blood for everyone. They move in when they sense an imbalance. They fill, as we say in capitalism, a niche. They are at their zenith. They are at their zenith now.

You think of all the things you've mistaken for ticks: crumbs, lint, other bugs, dimples, smears of chocolate, lentils, panthers, oboes, ciphers, masculinity, as well as a boneless chicken breast, lustiness, the 25th amendment, and yachts. And anonymity. Ticks are the burnt remains of forests. They are black holes. Vantablack™. They suckle the light of the world. You are not like them. Are you?

Night has fallen and the light in the small room is yellow. You stand in front of the mirror and see something small crawling on your bare shoulder. Flick it into the sink and rinse it down the drain, bang the door on your way out. You will deal with this later. You have dealt with it "now." You will "deal." With "it." In "time."

Think of a time you loved yourself. You are breathing the breath of those with whom you think you share nothing in common. Humidity on your face like a lace of fruit flies. It rained and you left the car windows open all night. Again. How does it end? Forever and ever. You are strangely calm, outside in the post-storm quiet, alone with your private hungers now. Anonymous, and questing.

# HERE (LIFE)

# Deborah Kaskinen Crandell
## *Taking Turns: A Collective American Portrait*

At eight a.m., I punch in and walk over to a checkout lane donning my cashier shirt and thinking how it seems like just months ago that I had been on the other side of the steel and rubber grocery belt. It really had been three years since forced retirement, then divorce and no one to rely on but myself. I look at the other cashiers wearing thick makeup, and tri-focals. Some had been professionals until they'd torn up their backs or had a birthday. We were all alike.

I would remain anonymous, standing behind a cash register, working for minimum wage. Customers began rushing the checkout lanes with shopping carts packed with purchases; People magazine, the Times, antacids, Preparation H, Depends, along with Hallmark cards meticulously, carefully, selected for loved ones faraway. Moose Tracks ice cream and chocolate syrups to be consumed while writing meaningful notes for loved ones far away to drop in the mail today. I watch their faded blue eyes look away into nowhere. "I'm retired and I just don't have enough money. Everything is so expensive. I wasted so much when I was young," said an elderly man. "Now the wife is ill and I'm flipping burgers."

Another man steps up badly crippled. "I used to be a pharmacist. I went white water rafting five years ago. My wife told me not to. I should've listened to her," he said as I bag his groceries.

Like Bonsai trees, with backs are bent, they limp forward with silver canes, looking sideways at others wearing wigs and pearls, or Viet Nam Vet baseball hats, they half smile, and they seem to travel in packs, wearing whiskered faces with deep set eyes and lines permanently etched into tanned Florida faces. A man dressed in neon orange and yellow plastic sheets pinned together covering just half his body was next in line. "I'm allergic to fabric and can't wear clothes," he explains as his wife nods in agreement.

I watch and imagine them as puppies with their round faces and bellies bulging over belt buckles in pastel polo shirts; or Dalmatians in polka dots. "What does the world want next of us?" asks a small bearded man. He throws his change on the belt for his coffee and waltzes out the door into the rain.

An overweight gentleman lowers his eyes and whispers as he hands me a brown paper bar, "Two cherry fritters. There was another but I already ate it. It's illegal to eat it and then pay isn't it?" I shrug and put his money in the drawer, waving him on.

At noon the blue collars arrive, fresh from the road repairs, wearing once white t-shirts now stained. Their arms are filled with bags of chips, gator aid and oranges, monster drinks, iced tea and gallons and gallons of water. Their eyes blur as they gaze off into the distance while reaching into their faded blue jeans and pay with cash, silently, then disappear quickly outdoors.

By twelve thirty, the nurses, aides and doctors rush in for sushi, dried fruit, and salads, wearing big watches, nametags, lanyards and key fobs. With faces pale from inside work, they tap to pay quickly on the UPC reader before racing back to work.

Lunch rush over, their white shirts and black pants spotted with sauces of different colors, the restaurant servers and cooks pause to explain the help didn't show up. Always in motion, they grab supplies they've run out of; flour or ground beef and then pay for their own food with food stamps or Snap cards, and then fly out the door.

The young mothers and a few fathers alone quietly arrive next, around two o'clock, just before school's out, bringing babies nicely dressed in stylish secondhand clothes. They pay for cereal and milk, with WIC cards, and sometimes credit cards that are denied. A young mother walks up smiling with her two boys and a dozen boxed donuts. The boys help stack the ice cream and gourmet cookies on the belt from a shopping cart filled with junk food. "We're celebrating that our divorce is final," she laughs.

By three o'clock the unemployed and homeless arrive. Their t-shirts read like newspapers; NRA, Ducks Unlimited, I Voted for Trump, Make America Great Again, Alabama Mud Dyed, Always Fresh and Never Frozen, Canadian Friends for over Two Hundred Years, and I'm a Suicide Risk. They ask for paper bags to be filled with beer, Vodka, Gin, Jack Daniels or Bourbon in bottles signed with gold ink sometimes already opened. They pay with cash, sometimes loose change or once all in quarters; "Before my brother died yesterday, he gave me this bag of quarters and said go and have a drink on me. I know he would have wanted me to do this." Coins still warm from his hands, I take them and let them fall into the drawer.

The late afternoon pre-dinner rush begins with a storm of hangry eyed teenagers buying snacks before sports practice. Sushi, broiled chickens, Beanie Babies, Hot Wheels, gum, and wine; all purchases of working parents while watching their Apple wristwatches and paying with half on a credit card and half in cash which they remove from designer wallets and purses are next. "We're all just slaves," says a woman who pauses and looks into my eyes as she purchases her wine.

A woman with brown cropped hair rushed in speaking loudly. "It was love at first sight! My yellow lab, their chocolate retriever... They went crazy when they saw each other. They were jumping on the windows. But it would never work, it is over five thousand dollars for AKC plus shots," she said aloud, mainly to herself. "I just came in for dog food and look at all I've got!"

Then the comfort dogs arrive with their masters making the connections that many humans can't seem to  anymore.

Once, people would pause and talk to each other, and affirm their identities. Now, most stand silently in long lines of stores filled with every imaginable item you could wish for; Fresh Salmon from Alaska? Four kinds of tomatoes imported from Thailand, Mexico, Canada, Brazil? Barely looking at each other, they are survivors of a grand experiment. "I'd go nuts if I had to do your job every day. Thank you for working," said a tall man in his gear ready for the gym.

I watch the clock, feet swollen from standing in one place all day. It is nearly time to punch out. A woman appears who peers at me closely. "My great great aunt was burned as a witch," she calmly states as she purchases a National Geographic featuring witchcraft. A few minutes later, a man with a dark black beard buys just a loaf of bread. "My ancestors were witch hunters," he states as he looks deeply into my eyes and then takes his bag and walks out of the store.

"Did your penance for the day?" asks the red-haired woman who'll replace me at the register.

"Your turn," I say. " It's my time to check out...."

# Chris Giroux
## *Art History*

### Christmas Portrait

My brother and I pulled silver branches from paper sleeves like swords from scabbards. We traced around cookie cutters to free stars, angels, gingerbread families from red, green, yellow construction paper. Our Advent chains garlanded the tree's branches, the entire upstairs bedroom. With glitter, ribbons, stickers from a school fundraiser (glue coating tongues), we deemed our work ready for JL Hudson's storefront displays.

Despite their non-holiday focus, we kept up the watercolors done by an alcoholic aunt: the first was of her Havanese, Tammy, who sometimes shared her beer; in the other, Winnie the Pooh studied a five-petaled daisy, cherry red. These images are now lost, so too my aunt's pen-and-ink drawings decorating my grandparents' den. Those were real masterpieces: the *Joy* of Fishtown, the *Janice Sue*, green hulls and gray cabins rising out of dark water.

### Landscape with Tree

St. Norbert's lacked a dedicated art teacher, so in Sunday school, I scissored away at egg cartons, added wisps of straw, and created an instant cradle for a plastic Baby Jesus. In second grade, when reading aloud (was it *Little House on the Prairie? Stuart Little?*), Mrs. Parker paused to show off Garth Williams' illustrations. She raised the book, panning the room just like Father Pettit with the host at mass. We listened, chapter by chapter, with old *Reader's Digests* before us. Page by page, we pulled loose each upper corner down to the gutter, created sharp creases with popsicle sticks. Eventually, Mrs. Parker helped us staple angled cover to angled cover; jokes and stories slanted into ski slopes, ruffled into pine trees. Then homeroom moms, armed with military-green spray paint, ushered us into the pregnant December air. Unlike balsams shipped south from Kalkaska, along rivers of Michigan concrete, mine stayed put. Mom, Grandma gave it two thumbs up.

## Color/Capital, 1976

We stored crayons, markers in a Hills Bros. can peddling patriotism; the White House, Lincoln Memorial, Capitol followed the curve of recycled tin. Removing the lid released a mix of coffee and wax, the random scrap of torn label. The 64-crayon box with built-in sharpener was a grandparents' gift I guarded. Each school year, I'd silently pray in Kmart's aisles, *Please, Mom, please, only Crayola.* Cornflower, copper, plum. Even then, I knew color captured cool.

## Palette, Grade School

My younger brother was the family artist, pulled from "regular school," and shuttled to Cherry Hill High for challenge math and cartoon drawing.

I got oil painting classes in Mrs. Scott's basement, trading Mom's check for time and canvas board.

A robin, slate sky, water pump, sand—my designs were heavy-handed, like a mix of turpentine and linseed oil.

At Utrecht's and JoAnn's, I marveled at paints, row upon row. Birthday money never went far enough. Mom, Dad always bought supplies—though sometimes just a single tube at a time.

I craved more. I learned, loved the texture, rhythm of shade, hue.

Cobalt. Umber and ochre. Crimson and vermilion.

The silent Mrs. Scott favored doing over explaining, showing over telling. With her liver-spotted hand placed over mine, she brought bristles to background; as one, we scraped the palette knife over rough surfaces to raise clouds.

Cerulean, titanium.

A field trip: in the Detroit Historical Museum, wooden forts became cobblestones became assembly lines; fleurs-de-lis flowered on flags. Old Mr. Klauke, whose dress shirts matched his socks, snuck us into the DIA; we rushed through the Rivera Court to Van Gogh's self-portrait near the gift shop. His straw hat glowed; his red-gold beard blossomed into a wheatfield you could swim through; searing eyes followed me out of the museum.

Im-press-shun-is-um.

## Light, Shadow, or Oils in a Blue Tackle Box (Junior High)

When Mrs. Scott retired, Mrs. Weed (two towns over)— her hair sometimes permed, sometimes the color of golden beets—let me sit in her adult oil painting class on a trial basis. She said I could call her Sandy, but I just silently raised my hand for help.

Each Monday, we worked in the paneled-off portion of her basement. Artist lights pointed in different directions, their silver bowls like haloes, brown extension cords like climbing snakes. In this Eden, we inhaled solvent, brush cleaner, Tide, All. I came to see the truth of moonbeams in the paint-by-number of Gethsemane in the school library—to see sunlight at Van's Beach streaking through clouds over Lake Michigan.

We realized my cadmium red and yellow ran because they were really watercolors. With her laugh like an Op Art puzzle, Mrs. Weed cried, "Oh, mixed media!"

### Sacrifice

Mrs. Weed played "I've Got a Gal in Kalamazoo," "Don't Sit Under the Apple Tree," and other oldies because Led Zeppelin led to head banging, too much fun: art required sacrifice.

She had us paint on glass before Christmas, to plan for images in reverse. A black-capped chickadee finally emerged from beige, grey, white paints and India ink; for a background, I clipped green and yellow ferns from velveteen wallpaper samples. Though pleased with the result, I gifted it to Grandma.

After each class, Dad raced us home, in the curved darkness of our grey Pinto, to catch the last fifteen minutes of *M\*A\*S\*H*.

I promised to keep my grades up.

### Negative Space, 10th Grade

Private lessons ended once art was a graduation requirement. Ms. Madry, of the cropped hair and oversized metal frames, expected total silence. Hands clenched at her sides, she'd march from the back room, where seniors coiled clay: "People! Drawing on the right side of the brain—it's the nonverbal lobe—means no talking, NO talking, NO TALKING."

Each chatting offender earned everyone (everyone!) drawings of shoes for homework. I became master of, slave to Mom's moccasins, Dad's wingtips, my sister's saddle shoes. I posed cowboy boots, Keds and Converse knockoffs, slippers and heels, sometimes alone, sometimes paired. They often appeared overturned or on their sides, like roadkill. Raiding closets, I sieved through shadows under beds and finished off fine-tip after fine-tip.

We eventually moved from continuous line drawings to stools wedged into and angling out of ladders, the tendrils of spider plants arcing earthward. When we inched away from negative space to the third eye, cupid's bow, I chose from photographs snapped in our basement or in the dining room, galley kitchen of my grandparents' Leland rental. Ms. Madry proclaimed progress; my faces weren't replicas, but realistic. Chiaroscuro, chroma. Gradation. Vanishing point.

## Saturation, Grad School

In college, art meant English, French, German texts. One spring break, in the Orangérie's lower level, waterlilies filled the frame of my Pentax K1000. Drowning in violet and azure, surrounded by humming heat vents, I anchored myself with pencil and paper, a new notebook. A guard nodded approval.

My mind swam back to the Sleeping Bear and Whaleback: the palette of green, gold, grey; campfire smoke like incense; sand like forgiveness. I imagined my grandfather, now buried next to my grandmother in St. Hedwig's Cemetery, wading through lake shadow. He pointed towards the horizon, South Manitou, invisible lighthouses. Then he dove—I just held my nose and ducked below—silencing the wind, slap of wave.

Baptized by beauty, immersed in water, word, and image, I never wanted—want—to surface.

# Susan F. Glassmeyer
## *Writing Is a Transformative Act of Generosity*

### At 9

Sister Thomas Rita lined our fourth-grade chalkboard ledge with several different Saturday Evening Post magazine covers. Glued to cardboard so they stood at attention, the depictions were often colorful Norman Rockwell paintings of family life in America. Sister was masterful at teaching us how to build a compelling paragraph. *If you can write a sensible five-sentence paragraph about one of these pictures, you can write a bigger story someday, perhaps even a book. And if you are very clever, you can make one small paragraph into a fine poem. In any case, it will be a gift to others!* Amazingly, some of us chose the same picture to write a narrative paragraph, yet each of our small stories was uniquely different from anyone else's. My young world blossomed.

### At 13

In 1963, my first published poem was accepted by my high school magazine, The Green Blazer. Our freshman English teacher told me it would be a comfort and a kindness to others if I would read *Riderless Horse with Boots Reversed* at a school memorial service honoring President John F. Kennedy. I learned how words could help us grieve.

## At 25

It was a naïve submission. Word by word I painstakingly typed up five of my handwritten poems on my new Smith-Corona typewriter. I slid the untitled, unfolded poems into a large manila envelope and delivered myself to an editor, a woman, a poet in Pawtucket, Rhode Island, our smallest state. Her reply was quick and unmerciful. The sharp point of her red pen scratched curt opinions across the face of my first cover letter. *Fold poems! They won't break! Your spelling is sloppy. Use some punction* (she meant punctuation). *Whatever happened to capitalization?* (I was influenced by e.e. cummings) *I* (she circled the word "I") *publish with titles!*

She said nothing about my poems, the heart of them—the blue jay that flew into the window breaking its neck, my father who chased me with a belt, the metaphorical campfires that burned in the foggy night keeping me alive. I said *forget it!*—a title to myself in capital letters. It will be a long time before anyone sees my poems again. I continued to write, in secret, for 15 years.

## At 40

The founder of a writing school for women where I lived said others needed to hear our words. She assured us that sharing art was an act of generosity, a way to build community that was healing for the writer as well as the reader and listener.

## Buried Alive

An old woman farmer
wakes up wise. She has labored
so long in this field
she no longer calls it work.

With a will toward dirt and darkness
she drops to her knees
at the first sight
of underground movement.

It is a child, of course—
assumed lost,
insoluble all these years,
though singularly whole.

Free of guilt, the girl
waves in her hand
a drawing of the moon,
fully expecting to be found.

## At 52

I was juried into a weeklong poetry workshop offered annually by Marge Piercy at her home on Cape Cod. There were ten of us. I was the only one without a degree in English or Creative Writing and I felt out of place. In a private tutorial in her garden gazebo, Marge warned me against getting an MFA. *They will ruin your voice, and your voice needs to be heard. Don't hold back!* Something changed in me that week and I was imbued with a greater sense of responsibility and purpose as a writer.

## At 67

I had just returned from a heart-opening international psychospiritual seminar on the east coast. How could we give of ourselves to the world in ways that also nourished ourselves in the process? I recommitted myself to my devotion to writing and promised to pay attention to opportunities to engage with the world. What would it be like to give without expecting anything in return? How would that action inform my writing and be of service to others?

While I was away at the seminar, a beloved elderly friend back home died unexpectedly. On the heels of my return, I drove across town in time to attend her funeral service. At the end of the freeway exit ramp stood a disheveled, homeless man on crutches, one leg poorly bandaged. He carried a handwritten sign: *Jobless. Children to feed.* He was looking furtively at drivers for a bit of money. I was feeling full-on open-hearted and had a surplus of cash leftover from my travels. I waved a $50 bill out the car window. He hobbled over to receive it, his eyes widening at the amount I offered. It felt natural to share the abundance that I had, although I'd never before given that much money to a beggar. We made brief but meaningful eye contact and smiled at each other. He God-blessed me and I slowly drove on.

When I looked back at him in my rear-view mirror, I saw him toss his crutches down the hill under the overpass. He was literally skipping around exuberantly, having conned me by his fake act. I had been utterly fooled by this man, but in that instance I felt no annoyance or anger. In fact, I broke up laughing at the whole thing and quickly found peace with the fact that I'd made someone very happy. In effect, I had made the lame walk again, and that was something to write about!

# Richard Kooyman
## *Time, Space, and Money*

I t is January in Michigan and I am looking out my studio window at the white that has covered the field and trees, giving me pause to think about how I came to be an artist.

Over time I have learned there are three essential things that any artist needs to succeed. *Time-* to be able to make work, a *space* -to be able to make work, and *money-* to survive and build an art practice.

I didn't always realize these were crucial to surviving as an artist. In 1982, eager and fresh out of graduate school, I moved to Frankfort, a small northern town on Lake Michigan, to work in a small wooden boat shop and continue my art practice.

After a couple of summers, the small boat shop folded. I got another job at a local lumber yard but with each new job, I felt further away from the art world I wanted to be in. I didn't have a dedicated studio space and made do with an extra bedroom in my rental house, but working in a bedroom that says *bedroom* every time I entered began to erode my drive to make art. Weekday nights working in the dimly lit bedroom studio turned into weekends. I was struggling to stay connected to art. Struggling to financially make ends meet. Struggling to still be able to call myself an artist.

Desperately wanting a more committed art practice. in 1989 I applied for a grant from the National Endowment for the Arts. To complete the application I needed to have 20 slides of my current work. I didn't have my own photographic equipment so I had to hire a professional photographer. The complete application was then mailed in to be reviewed by a national group of professional working artists and gallerists.

After several months I received a very governmental-looking letter in the mail. I nervously opened it to read that I had been awarded a grant for $5000. My mind was reeling with new possibilities. $5000 was more money than my bank account had ever seen. The grant gave me the confidence to search for and commit to a dedicated studio space, which I did find. It was small, only 400 square feet, with a tiny basement window, but it was my first real studio. Someone suggested I do an up-and-coming art fair in a wealthy suburb of Cleveland, Ohio. I didn't have gallery representation at the time, and art fairs were not that common. I knew very little about what they entailed but I took the risk. I took some of the grant money to buy an outdoor pop-up tent, build a plywood display, and I bought a 1982 Dodge pickup for $1500. I loaded the truck with everything and drove 8 hours to the two-day event. I remember going back to my Motel 6 room, counting the money, and jumping up and down on the bed to the sum of $2000, throwing the bills into the air. Later that summer I got into the Ann Arbor Art Fair, the biggest art fair in my home state. I couldn't believe it when I sold almost everything I brought with me. With the same body of work I applied to and got accepted by Objects Gallery, an established Chicago gallery. I finally saw that I might be able to be a full-time artist and I took another risk. I quit my job at the lumber yard.

Had I not received the financial assistance from the NEA grant, along with its peer recognition, I might not have continued making art.. The grant was a symbolic connection to a body of working artists across the country, and it gave me the seed money to be able to build my art practice. It revitalized me.

In 1989, the year I received my grant, Ronald Reagan was leaving office, replaced by George H. W. Bush. Conservative politicians like Jessie Helms from North Carolina had been attacking the NEA for grants given to artists they considered offensive.

Over the years I followed these political attacks and began to research the history of the NEA. I learned that in 1963 President John F. Kennedy gave a speech at Amherst College shortly before he was assassinated. In that speech, he said:

> I see little more importance to the future of our country...than full recognition of the place of the artist... Society must set the artist free to follow his vision where it takes him... And the nation which disdains the mission of art invites...the fate of having nothing to look backward to with pride and nothing to look forward to with hope.

President Kennedy believed not only in the importance of the arts but in the individual artists' role in society. His vision, some say it was Jackie Kennedy's, planted the seed for what would become, under President Johnson, the National Endowment for the Arts.

For the next 25 years, the NEA would continue to grow and support new and established artists with direct, no-strings-attached grants. But the future of the NEA Artists Grants would not survive.

The Republican campaign to eliminate the NEA, which was coined the culture wars, not only attacked funding the NEA but also the character and artistic ideas of those who were deciding how the funds were being spent, and the artists themselves. The conservative right framed the source of contemporary art as decadent and corrupt, urban and elitist, while their preference for populist art was centered in the heartland and based on simple values and purity.

In 1997 then-Senate Majority Leader Dick Armey (R) of Texas would become the face of the aggression against the NEA. During a House subcommittee meeting, he testified that the NEA should be defunded.

The NEA no longer awards grants to visual artists. Shortly after Armey's testimony, the NEA succumbed to the political pressure from the Right. The endowments appropriation was slashed and it stopped awarding grants to individual visual artists completely. Today the NEA's meager appropriation goes to art institutions and arts organizations on the state and local level, depriving artists of direct assistance.

Stay with me, it gets even weirder. The NEA and the Michigan Arts and Culture Council doesn't even use the word *artist* in its mission statement any longer.

Over the years I have questioned what is lost when art is attacked by a destructive political ideology. I get angry that the program I benefited so much from, that offered me the time, space, and money to grow as an artist in society was destroyed by politicians and individuals who knew little to nothing about art, making decisions as if they did. I worry that the word *artist* is being erased out for the ubiquitous sounding word *creative*.

I fear what we have lost is the very seed Kennedy planted when he started the National Endowment for the Arts. We have lost the understanding, that art, poetry, music, theater, and dance provides us with *the basic human truth which must serve* as *the touchstone of our judgment*. Once that is lost, will we ever get it back?

# Nora Liu Robinson
## *Perfection: My So-Called Dream*

'm sitting on a small, wooden chair at a small, wooden table under the window in my little brother's bedroom for two reasons: (1) There's a kid-sized table and chairs perfect for my kid-sized body, and (2) My parents are making me.

I'm here because my story was chosen for a program called Young Authors. Because I'm in fourth grade and wasn't born yesterday, I know it's a big deal. At my school, McKinley Elementary, only two stories will be showcased at Young Authors–and "My So-Called Dream" is one of them.

To make my book, I used my school's "publishing center." On the bottom half of every page, I drew my illustrations. On the top half, I wrote the words in very light pencil. All that's left is to trace over the pencil with a pen, erase the pencil marks, and make it final–the way my book will be forever.

And I've tried. Honestly. It's just that every time I sit down to write, the time is up before I know it, and there are so many pages left to trace. With my dad at work and my mom busy with my kid brother, nobody stops me from playing Nintendo Super Spike V'Ball with my sister instead of writing.

Which brings me to today. Even though it's Saturday, my parents said I can't do anything–ANYTHING–until I finish this book. My dad even brought the tripod and the large video recorder upstairs.

"We will know," my dad said, loosening the tripod legs and planting them into the plush carpet near the door, "that you have been working because we are going to watch the tape." He lifted the heavy black video recorder from its case, plugged it into the wall, and carefully perched it on the tripod, pointing at the waiting penciled pages and me.

From where I sit, I turn around to look at the camera. I know my parents aren't there, but I feel watched. I turn back to the table and pick up my pen. Downstairs I hear my sister and brother playing, and hear my dad watching the game. I trace a word and lean back to examine it. *Nice,* I think, *but could be better.*

My five college roommates and I gather around the TV in an overpriced rental home in Ann Arbor. I don't actually live here—well, I do now. I graduated with an English degree last spring, but I'm regrouping. I spend my days driving from house to house as a private English tutor, and I spend my nights hostessing at a chain restaurant. I've known most of these roommates for four years, and they let me pay $100 a month for a futon in their living room.

One of my roommates, Lily, has suggested a home movie night where each of us shows a video clip of a "quintessential moment." The idea is that after living together for some years, we want to let each other know that "we've always been this way." Some of us sit on my bed/futon, some sit on the other futon, and some sit on the floor. Lily's video highlights herself as a child in a ballet class. As the children follow the instructor through exercises, Lily, a born leader, keeps stepping away from the bar to reposition the girl ahead of her.

I'm not sure how I remembered my tape exists, but when my turn comes, I pop it into the VCR and settle back onto my futon.

A smaller Nora comes into view, maybe nine years old. We see her sitting at a small table facing wallpapered woodland creatures in the browns and oranges that characterized the 70's and 80's. Positioned at her four o'clock, the camera shows much of her back and a little of her right side. She hunches over a piece of paper, right hand holding a Bic Cristal ballpoint pen. On the table to her right sits an eraser and a bottle of liquid Wite-Out.

My roommates look eager as we watch nine-year-old Nora put pen to paper. She writes for a few seconds, then sits back. She looks up out the window, then down at her paper. Her right hand slowly moves toward the Wite-Out. She shakes the bottle, staring at her paper the whole time, then unscrews the cap and removes the little brush.

This video is excruciating; nothing is happening. I look nervously at my roommates. Maybe I should've chosen a video of the high-school me sprinting the pants off my opponents in the 400-meter dash. My roommates watch the TV closely, though, smiling. They anticipate something.

The nine-year-old Nora on screen carefully brushes the offending letter a fresh white and replaces the cap. She pauses a moment to read the Wite-Out label, then turns it to read the back. She sets it down and blows on her paper. She waves it dry with her hand and turns around to glance at the camera. She looks like she's considering something. Then nine-year-old Nora turns back to the table and picks up the pen, writes for a moment, examines the paper, examines the pen, and looks out the window.

For some time, she repeats this ritual. We watch her do anything but ink in a final draft of a book. Then, without warning, Nora throws her pen on the table and launches to her feet. We only see the backs of her knees until she turns around and marches to the video camera. She crouches as she walks, so that by the time she arrives, her smooth face is already directly at camera height. Transfixed, I take in the skin unmarked by acne and the brows untweezed. Her round, brown eyes stare deep into the camera's eye—our eyes, *my* eyes—and she says simply, "I'm a perfectionist. That means I like everything perfect." Her small voice is matter-of-fact. And just like that, she spins and we watch the backs of her knees recede from the camera until she slips back into the wooden chair as if nothing has happened.

My roommates erupt into laughter; they lean into each other, double forward, fall off chairs. Beth manages to squeak, "That is *so* you!" I laugh along, pleased that I did indeed select the right quintessential video.

Decades will pass before I realize the full weight of that declaration. But in this moment, a small awareness blooms. College for me has been nothing but sitting alone at a desk at three o'clock in the morning, staring at a blank computer screen and spending what feels like an hour to write three words, and taking another hour to delete one. My college self is not so different from that child on the screen. What my parents found exasperating then and my roommates find hilarious now is, in fact, an integral part of my personality and identity.

Though chasing perfection certainly presents challenges, it's a dream that continues to lure. Just as I can't seem to begin any creative project that is important to me, I also can't seem to live my life without one. Perfectionism, I've come to understand, is part of my ongoing urge to create. I've found a supportive community of understanding writers, and I'm learning strategies to harness my perfectionism in productive ways. And so I continue to sit here—under a window, on a bigger chair at a bigger table—and write.

# CONTRIBUTORS

**Nicole Bernadette Birkett** (she/her) graduated with a BA in English from Michigan State University. She works supporting organizing and membership efforts for public school unions, raises sheep and goats with her husband, leads the Ludington Writers, and is editor in chief of Making Waves: A West Michigan Review. Her work has appeared in publications such as *Peninsula Poets, Variety Pack*, and MSU's *Offbeat* and *OATS*. Learn more at LudingtonWriters.org or @nbbirkett.

**Jeanne Blum Lesinski** writes poetry and prose in a wide variety of styles and for many audiences. Her work has appeared in journals, anthologies, and online for many years. She is best known for her middle-grade biography of Microsoft founder Bill Gates for A&E but is most proud of her poetry collection, *Tethers End*, published in 2023 by Shanti Arts. With long roots in Cheboygan County where her mother grew up, she enjoys alternating stays between the family farm there and her home in Saginaw. When not engrossed in a writing or art project, she may be found on a trail, in a garden, or on the water.

**Michelle Boyer** spent 27 years teaching writing in Ohio public schools. She lives with her husband, Ed, in Petoskey, Michigan, where she volunteers, bringing together arts and community.

**Barbara Heydenberk Brose's** professional work has been published by museums in Cleveland, Ohio; Toronto, Canada; Gastonia, North Carolina;, and Ann Arbor, Michigan. At the same time she has (more privately) been writing poems. She is now revising some of them and creating new ones. Her first poetry submission was accepted by the Mackinac Island Arts Council for its "Poetic Visions of Mackinac" exhibit; she was elated. In her work—often partly-titled Same Life—she explores decades of observation.

**Roberta Brown's** work publications include local newspapers, Peninsula Poets, Panoplyzine, and online at Michigander's Post and Short Fiction Break. She served as President of Detroit Working Writers from 2017 to 2021 and is a Poetry Editor for the MacGuffin. She is currently the 2023-2024 Royal Oak Artist Laureate.

**Diana Burton** was born in Denver, Colorado. She went to Indiana for college at Anderson University. She received her Masters in Religious Education and a Masters of Divinity at Anderson University Seminary. She served churches in Ohio, Indiana, and Michigan with her husband. After his death, she retired from chaplaincy and being a manager at Beaumont Hospital in Royal Oak. She moved north to Northport and have since moved to Traverse City with her husband, whom she met during COVID. She has one son, Jacob, and his partner, Evan, is like another son to her.

**Rosemarie Canfield** lives in Buckley, MI, with her husband on a forty acre farm where they raised their nine children . She has been publish in "Poets Night Out" in Traverse City. She also has a larger piece publish in Marrow Mag, "Invisible," that was nominated for the Push Cart Prize, another published piece in Sad Girls Club, "Creating an Intentional World," and her story "Pilgrim" is part of the anthology, *After: Stories About Loss & What Comes Next*. She is currently working on gathering the fragments of her life's rich experiences into a memoir.

**Carrie Cantalupo Sharp** writes poetry and flash fiction and has been published in *Pike's Peak, Poets Night Out, Making Waves, You Might Need to Hear This, Poetry Project Matters* and *The Closed Eye Open*. She is currently working on a hybrid chapbook. Carrie lives in Maple City in the Bohemian Wood and loves to hike, travel and read.

**Judy Childs** is a poet and retired Special Education teacher. She began writing in the late 1990s, taking classes from Ferris and Grand Valley and began to love writing. She journals and writes poetry. She has attended the Interlochen Writer's Summer Retreat for the past eight years. She finds submitting work to be both a thrill and a lesson in rejection. As Ray Bradbury said, "Accept rejection. Reject acceptance."

As a retired teacher of 32 years at Kaleva Norman Dickson Schools where she taught Art and English, wrote grants and designed outreach programs earning national recognition, **Deborah Kaskinen Crandell** is excited to pursue my interests in writing and illustrating children's books, poetry, and participating in shows locally, regionally and nationally. She loves traveling, spending time with her grandchildren and dogs, and the beach.

**Lynn Domina** is the author of several books, including three collections of poetry: *Inland Sea, Framed in Silence,* and *Corporal Works.* Her individual poems have been published in many periodicals and anthologies, including *Lake Effect, About Place, The Christian Century, The New England Review,* and others. She teaches English at Northern Michigan University and serves as Creative Writing Editor of *The Other Journal.* She lives in Marquette, Michigan, along the beautiful shores of Lake Superior.

**Kathleen Dunckel** is a family physician, recently retired after 30 years with Alcona Health Centers. She and her husband raised two daughters on an old 76-acre family farm in Alcona County. She wrote her first poem after her mother died in October 2018.

**Rhonda Sider Edgington** is a professional classical musician (a performer, educator, and church musician) who enjoys writing for many of the reasons she enjoys music making, because through it she can communicate with others and express what's happening inside herself. She is the Music Director and Organist at Hope Church in Holland, Michigan, teaches at Calvin University, and is a frequent performer throughout Michigan as well as around the US as a soloist, and with the groups Great Lakes Duo (organ and trumpet) and Thunder & Wind (organ and percussion). In addition, she writes a monthly column on music for the *Holland Sentinel*, and with a friend facilitates a poetry corner for their church's newsletter, highlighting members' poetry. She lives in Holland with her husband and two teenagers, where she loves walking the beaches and trails around Lake Michigan, riding her bike, visiting the Holland farmer's market, and reading when she should be doing something more productive.

**John Flesher** retired in 2023 after a 42-year career as an Associated Press journalist. For more than three decades he was based in Traverse City, covering environmental issues and general news in Michigan's northern Lower Peninsula and Upper Peninsula. He served as AP's Great Lakes reporter and was a member of the news cooperative's Global Environment Team, covering national stories including the Deepwater Horizon oil spill in the Gulf of Mexico, Great Plains floods and Western wildfires. He was awarded a Ted Scripps Fellowship in Environmental Journalism at the University of Colorado and numerous fellowships from the Institute for Journalism and Natural Resources. Earlier, he was posted in Washington, D.C., and Raleigh, North Carolina. Flesher has written freelance articles for *Traverse Magazine* and literary essays for *Dunes Review.* He's a member of Michigan Writers and has twice attended the Bear River Writers' Conference. He is husband to Sharon Perkinson Flesher and father of

Dylan and Leah. He enjoys reading, listening to Bach and the Beatles, hiking northern Michigan's trails, and wines from near and far.

**Mary Bevans Gillett** is the executive director for the Northwest Michigan Arts & Culture Network, a regional arts services organization dedicated to supporting and strengthening the collective power of artists, culture bearers, arts and cultural organizations, the creative sector and vibrant communities throughout northern lower Michigan. A member of Michigan Writers, she has been a frequent contributor to regional publications including the *Traverse City Record-Eagle* and the *Traverse City Business News*, and regular participant at Interlochen Center for the Arts' annual Writers Retreat and the Writability Guild. From 2016-2024, Gillett led the Network's annual Northwest Michigan Arts & Culture Summit which helped plant the seeds for this *Transformational* anthology and the MACC Community Partners grant project.

**Susan F. Glassmeyer** is Codirector of the Holistic Health Center of Cincinnati, Ohio, where she works as a somatic therapist and Feldenkrais® Practitioner, helping people heal from trauma in order to experience the poetry of presence in their bodies. Susan grew up for part of her life outside of Detroit and considers northern Michigan (The Village of Empire) her home away from home for more than twenty years. Susan was named Ohio Poet of the Year for her 2018 collection *Invisible Fish* (Dos Madres Press). Her fifth and forthcoming book, *Please Treasure Yourself: Zen Poems*, will be published by Shanti Arts (Brunswick, Maine) in 2025. Susan's poems have appeared in *Rattle, JAMA, Naugatuck River Review, Dunes Review*, and other print and online journals. Susan traces the roots of her interest in both meditation and poetry to early childhood when her railroad worker grandfather taught her to pay close attention to the language of train whistles. Learn more at susanglassmeyer.com.

**Chris Giroux** teaches composition, creative writing and literature courses at Saginaw Valley State University. A reader for *Dunes Review*, his most recent chapbook is *Sheltered in Place* (Finishing Line Press).

**Laura Hunt** is retired from a long career of volunteer and paid service in the non-profit arena which included foster care, international health care and community development, grant writing, and teaching Art at a school for low-income girls in the inner city of Washington, DC. Laura and her husband split their time between Northern Virginia and Harbor Springs, Michigan.

**Richard Kooyman** lives and maintains a studio with his partner, the painter Melanie Parke, in NW Lower Michigan two miles from the 'big' lake as they like to say. Earning his MFA from Ohio State University he has been awarded a National Endowment for the Arts Artist Grant, a Michigan Arts Council Grant, and The Michigan Governor's Award in the Arts. He has also been an artist-in-residence at the Vermont Studio Center, The Heliker- LaHotan Foundation, The Antico Borgo Finocchieto in Tuscany, and a Visiting Artist at the American Academy in Rome. "I make paintings because I believe it is still one of the most important personal, social, and political acts a person can do."

**Kris Kunz** is a poet in northern Michigan. She lives in a small town near Lake Michigan with her husband, dog and horses.

**Alison Lake** was born and raised in Michigan and has lived here her whole life. She has a B.A. in poetry from Hope College and an MA in Literature and MFA in poetry both from Western Michigan University. She lives in central Michigan with her husband, only living child, and elderly black cat.

**Holly Lang:** explorer, collector of stories, finding joy to share.

**Candace Lee** was lucky enough to attend Interlochen one summer as a young oboist and Meadowbrook School of Music the summer before MSU. Writing workshops have been pivotal including the transformational focus recently with Anne-Marie Oomen. Her writing has appeared in *The Prepress Awards, Volume Two: Michigan Voices, The MacGuffin, Dunes Review, Black Buzzard Press/ Visions-International, Mankata Poetry Review, The Vincent Brothers, Sow's Ear Poetry Review, Double Reed, Walloon Writers Review.*

**Michelle Lucchesi** has been involved in the arts from an early age. Her dance, theater and writing experience includes five years with Inside Out Music and Dance in Midland Michigan, twenty years with Northeast Michigan Art Council in Standish Michigan as performing arts instructor, twenty years with Academy of Performing Arts in Alma Michigan as student and instructor, thirty years in community theater and church theater, where she has been vocalist, playwright, choreographer and director. Michelle has acted or directed in over twenty plays and written over thirty original scripts or adaptations for the stage, with one being published in 2004 in Standard Publishing's Easter Programs for the Church. She has been Artistic Director of My Turn Performing Arts

Collective since 2019. She has performed modern, ballet, tap, clogging, and a variety of social dances, and has taught and choreographed creative movement, musical theater and liturgical dance, and performed as a vocalist and musician for numerous performance over thirty years. As a generalist artist she is highly collaborative and integrative in modalities and loves to experiment in combining elements of various arts to see the power and surprise they can offer when they play off each other. She holds a Master's degree in Humanities and a Master's degree in Clinical Psychology. She has worked as a psychologist in Alma, Michigan, since 1996, and has published a creative non-fiction self-help book called *Fly on the Wall: Stories of Therapy for the Self Help Junkie*.

**Douglas P. Marsh** was born at Munson Medical Center in Traverse City, Michigan. Attended Elk Rapids High School followed by University of Michigan, earning a degree in philosophy. Struggled to find work in wake of 2008. Expatriated to SE Asia 2013-2018. Returned to the USA with a wife and daughter in 2018. Started writing professionally as a newspaper reporter in 2021. He currently writes full-time based in West Branch, Michigan.

**Sara Maurer** is a writer in Sault Ste. Marie, Michigan. Place deeply informs her writing, particularly how it influences identity and choice. Her work has appeared in *Hominum Journal, Dunes Review, The Twin Bill*, and others. She was selected as a 2023 Suzanne Wilson Artist-in-Residence at the Glen Arbor Art Center. Her debut novel is forthcoming in Winter 2026 from St. Martin's Press. Howland Literary represents her.

**Anne-Marie Oomen** received the Michigan Author for 2023-24. Her memoir, *As Long As I Know You: The Mom Book* won AWP's Sue William Silverman Nonfiction Award, a Silver IPPY, and a Michigan Notable Book Award. She wrote *Lake Michigan Mermaid* with Linda Nemec Foster, Love, Sex and 4-H , and many others. *The Long Fields*, a retrospective of new and selected essays, is her most recent. *Lake Huron Mermaid*, a sister book to *Lake Michigan Mermaid*, is forthcoming in fall of 2024.

**Marsha Jane Orr**, MS, MA, MEd is Founder and Vice President of Consulting at IntrepreneurCoaching.com. She is an organization change & development specialist with 10+ years of national and international experience integrating development strategies in academic & consulting organizations with start-ups and Fortune 500 clients. Prior to her employment with Mackinac Arts Council, Ms. Orr worked as associate faculty at Cornell University NYSLIR Extension, served as Director of Undergraduate Management Studies at Lesley University, Director of Labor Relations at University of Minnesota, and as a senior consultant at CSC Index, Cambridge, MA.

**Nora Liu Robinson** is a writer and teacher in Northern Michigan. Her essay "The Move" was published in *After: Stories about Loss & What Comes Next*. She was awarded the 2023 Indigo Author Diversity Scholarship for her current project, an essay collection exploring the pressures of immigration, motherhood, and generational trauma in a multicultural household.

**Vonni Sage** lives in northwest Michigan, finding creative inspiration everywhere. A tree hugger, natural building enthusiast, avid reader, and ukulele plunker, she can often be found wandering along beaches and in forests, collecting inspiration and writing stories.

**Melissa Seitz** is the author of the chapbook *Brain Aura Blues*, winner of the 2024 Michigan Writers Cooperative Press chapbook contest for creative nonfiction. Her work has appeared in *After: Stories About Loss & What Comes Next, The Bear River Review, The Dunes Review, The Lake, the Walloon Writers Review,* and other journals. She is a writer and a photographer who lives at Higgins Lake with her husband. As of July 23, 2024, she has photographed the sunrise 2,397 days in a row. She is currently revising her memoir *Lost in Time in Michigan*.

**Shelley Smithson** is a psychotherapist living and working in Elk Rapids, Michigan. She loves to write in her free time and finds the narratives of clients to be inspiring to her work as a poet. Her writing helps anchor her when the pain of others and the world seem too much. Poems of hers have appeared in *Walloon Writers Review, Rue Scribe, Door is a Jar, Passager Journal,* and *Poets Night Out Chapbook,* Traverse City. She loves to spend time with her family and friends and be engaged with her community. Roaming the beaches of northern Michigan is her way of cleansing and re-centering.

**Daniel Stewart** is a writer, writing coach, storyteller, and occasional book designer and radio producer. He has a Ph.D. in history, and writes memoir and fiction (while trying to keep them from overlapping), and is also a past president of Michigan Writers, Inc. He lives on an 1890s farmstead in Leelanau County, Michigan, with his wife and a number of animals, some of them invited.

**Minnie Wabanimkee** is a full-blood Odawa from northern Michigan. She is an award winning photographer, journalist, and artist, and has spent her lifetime documenting the life of Native people in the Midwest area. Her work has been exhibited in state and national museums, and publications, including *CONTEMPORARY GREAT LAKES POWWOW REGALIA "Nda Maamawigaami (Together We Dance)"* and several smaller publications. Minnie is a recipient of the Robert F. Kennedy Journalism Award for Excellence in Photojournalism.

**Ellen Welcker** is the author of *Ram Hands* (Scablands Books, 2018), *The Botanical Garden* (Astrophil Press, 2010), and five chapbooks, including *Keep Talking* (Sixth Finch Books, 2023). She is a newcomer to the US midwest and is online at ellenwelcker.com.

Made in the USA
Monee, IL
08 September 2024

64817692R00090